zuckerbook

Jerry Zucker Middle School of Science

The Zuckerbook Project

Spring 2020

Faculty Advisor

Mr. Erik J. Hilden

Copy Editing

Erik J. Hilden editor-in-chief
Jacob Jaycock copy editor
Alajah Thomson copy editor
Juelz Utreras Segundo copy editor
Ta'Kayliah-Prin Smart copy editor

Art Department

Andrea Ramirez Nunez creative director
Olivia Summerlin production artist & illistrator
Teandra Johnson production artist & illustrator
Morgan Howard production artist & illustrator

Social Media

I'ris Gudrunardottir social media lead
Tori Odom social media
Erick Hidalgo social media
Angela Gonzales Gomez social media

Marketing

Annabelle Lockridge marketing lead
Emory Rose fundraising
Yessica Morales Lira fundraising

Cover Art **Teandra Johnson**

Published by **The Zuckerbook Project,** ©2020, North Charleston, SC.

The Students of Jerry Zucker Middle School of Science
6401 Dorchester Road Room 159
North Charleston, South Carolina 29418
Principal: Jacob Perlmutter
Assistant Principal: Andrea Gadsden
Assistant Principal: Shorace Guider
They are our heroes.

ISBN: 978-0-578-71709-8

Printed in the United States of America.

Dedication

This work is dedicated to the students who created each piece that is contained within these pages.
Their words, their art, their spirits, and their energies bring this work to life.
May their voices always be heard.

Community Involvement

Endeavors such as these are evidence of the great things that can happen when a community pulls together in the face of adversity and produces a testament to the voices of their children. Without the support of our community, this would not have been possible, and without further support, future endeavors may not come to pass. We have had a lot of support this year, but we can always use more, as is true of any non-profit activity. If you are interested in donating to The Zuckerbook Project or are interested in volunteering to help in any way, please feel free to get in touch. I can be reached at **erik_hilden@charleston.k12.sc.us** or at the following address:

The Zuckerbook Project c/o
Jerry Zucker Middle School of Science
6401 Dorchester Rd. Room 159
North Charleston, SC 29418
843-767-8383 ext. 25614
or 503-778-0393. We look forward to hearing from you.

Acknowledgements

Each year, it seems, there are developments, advancements, setbacks, more setbacks, more advancements, and a lot of folly, and every year these fine students and this learning community do not fail to amaze me.

We had a leaner crew for Volume 12. No less dedicated, no less interested, and no less inspired, they worked tirelessly until everything shut down due to the COVID-19 Pandemic and ensuing quarantine. Then I had to pick up the pieces.

Community support is growing and it is that support that is bringing this project to your hands right now. Without our continuing supporters, none of this would be possible, but without our new supporters, we wouldn't be able to reach new heights. In their own way, everyone in this building, as well as people thousands of miles away, has made it possible to continue our work and break new ground.

These fine folks warrant special mention for their continuing support and dedication to the love of reading and writing.

Mr. Jacob Perlmutter, our esteemed principal, remains our loudest and most ardent supporter. His endless ideas for financially supporting The Zuckerbook Project, and helping us make them happen, are appreciated in more ways than any one of us can properly express. He has his eye on the prize. Thank you, sir, for having our backs. We are grateful.

Ms. Nikki Mustipher, Ms. Erin Presto, Ms. Katherine Sauter, Ms. Elizabeth Gleim, **Mr. Adam Bevins, Ms. Marian Gathers, and Ms. Amy Buckheister** provide connections to students that I could never acquire on my own, supportting us in the other wings of the school. Thank you, my friends. You rock.

Ms. Abbey Wroten our new art teacher, jumped right in and funneled a lot of excellent artwork our way. Her students are keeping up with the high standards set by her predecessors and we could not be more pleased. Many of their pieces of art are in this volume. Thank you so much for your support, Ms. Wroten, and welcome aboard!

The entire faculty and staff of Zucker Middle School has continued to tolerate our pleas for donations, financial support, and our fundraising activities. We are fortunate, indeed, and could not ask for a more supportive community at this school. Thank you. You are appreciated more than you will ever know.

Dr. Clark G. Hilden, who has continued to donate to our cause, deserves special mention, for donating large amounts of money and inspiration, support for our students, and mentoring as we go forward in the unchartered waters of small batch publishing. Take a look at his textbook, ***Uniquely Oregon***, if you want an interesting read about a fascinating state created by a dedicated teacher of geography. It is fun to read regardless of your interests, and available at Amazon.com.

Ms. Cynthia Hilden is an ongoing enthusiast of literature and reading, and her support for this issue is greatly appreciated. She is in no small part much of why I love writing and reading as much as I do and I remain grateful for that. Thank you so much. Your support means everything.

Ms. Jennifer Wicker at **The Circular Congregational Church** in Downtown Charleston helped us out with a significant donation. The support is much appreciated, Ms. Wicker. Thank you very much indeed.

Ms. Rhea Farmer and Ms. Esther Courtney made donations through GoFundMe.com, as well. It is a wonderful thing when the community at large jumps in to assist student projects and support student literacy. Thank you very much for donating!

Joshua Van Kall, manager of Sam's Club #8252 near Tanger Outlet Mall in North Charleston, South Carolina, orchestrated a grant through Walmart Community Grants to help us with our expenses this year. There is no measure to our gratitude for your support, and for the support of Walmart Community Grants. Thank you.

Mr. James Brooks retired at the end of the 2016-2017 school year and is sorely missed. His support for The Zuckerbook Project was unwaivering, and his assistance in assembling the best crew possible for each year was invaluable in setting the standards for this class and this publication. We remain in his debt and envious of his retirement.

Ms. Jordane Lotts and **Ms. Naquita Page-Dawson** have taken over the guidance department and have continued working with us to populate our crew with engaged, intelligent, and creative young minds who want to make a difference. Thank you both for your involvement. In the face of changing times and changing norms, we managed to pull it off.

Ms. Gina Harris and **Mr. Mike Harris** have repeatedly taken it upon themselves to promote The Zuckerbook Project by traveling the world and snapping prictures of Zuckerbook in the hands of children. A trip to Guatemala had them leave a copy in the hands of a young boy whose father began to teach him English by reading Zuckerbook. Unbelievable. Thank you.

Ms. Bridget Means and **Sage Design Studio** started helping us when Zuckerbook was produced on a laser printed and assembled with a stapler. She brought us out of the "obviously school made" realm into the world of the professional look, working with us to create a brand identity and dedicating her design studio to each issue of Zuckerbook twice per year at an unheard of discount. There is no way to thank her for her work other than to say that without her, we wouldn't be here.

Ms. Sarah Callahan remains, and always shall remain, a spirit guide on our journey. Zuckerbook started, in part, because of her, and though she is taking time off from teaching to raise a family, she remains within the pages of this book. Bless her and the work that she does. She is a jewel in the crown of education and teaching.

And, to each of you, as always, thank you. This book is as much for you as the students and communty with which we work, and we remain grateful for your involvement. Thank you for deciding that Zuckerbook is worthy of support, thank you for purchasing our books and thank you for believing in our project. Without you, the energy to continue might not exist. We are grateful for your support, for you are the people who will spread the word, and will bring us into the front lines of young adult literature. Your support is valued beyond measure and drives our dedication to the process. It is, after all, the process, right?

The Mission of The Zuckerbook Project is, and shall remain, to produce the very highest quality student publication of literary works intermingled with visual art, while remaining faithful to the Zucker Middle School student experience, and then distribute it to the community, so that our voices may be heard. Let them always be heard.

Open it and read...

-- Mr. Erik J. Hilden, June 6th, 2020

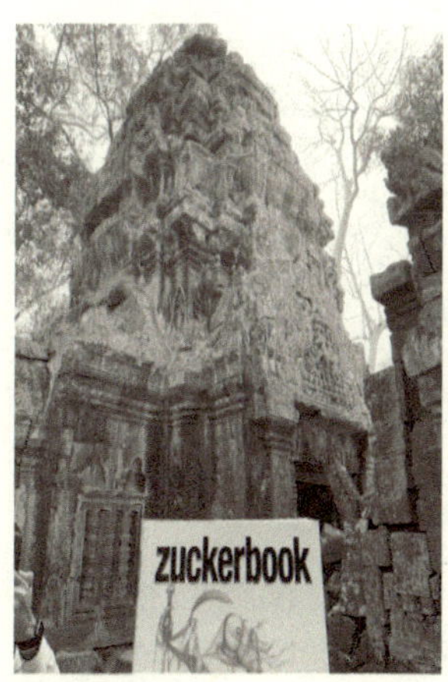

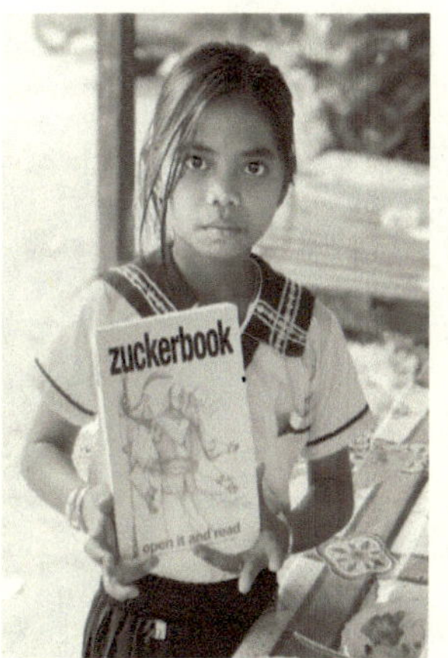

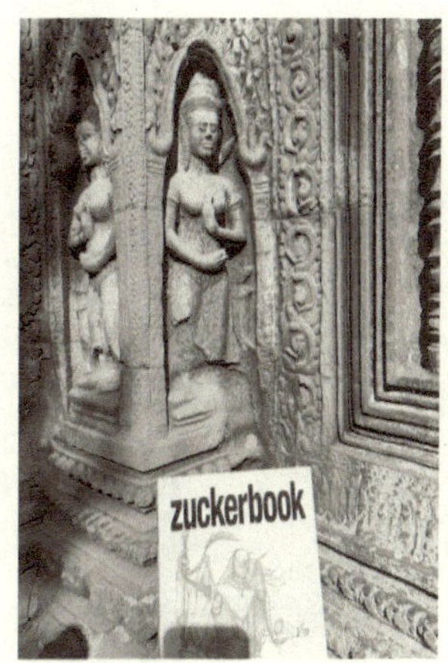

Zuckerbook in Cambodia.

photos by Gina Harris

zuckerbook

Contents

Prologue

Since a prologue is, by nature, a way of introducing the book and letting the reader shake its hand, we thought we would write another one. There are always plenty of surprises.

How to introduce each chapter is, as you can well imagine, not so simple a task. But, because we are The Zuckerbook Project and insist on doing things our own way, here they are.

Angry Little Birds runs the gamut from heartbreak and crisis to dukes-up conflict. Every one of us is a star, and here is our moment to shine.

No Guard Rail brings us to the edge of reason. Pushing envelopes in ways that only teenagers can, our writers decided that the time for being polite had passed.

Mysterious Equation delves into the depths of mathematics and matters of the heart, extending the metaphor of mathematics and cold calculations into the spectrum of teen love.

Chemically Speaking brings the reader full circle into the scientific world of what makes the teen heart tick. And tock. And tick. And tock. Ad nauseum.

The Fruit of Injustice – addressing the ideologies of revolution and protest, our writers took their very best swing at the core of injustice in America and at school.

Exclamation Points is a collection of poems as shouting. Every now and again, it is good to let loose.

Oppression Session continues our annual interpretations of *Reading Lolita in Tehran* and *Persepolis*, offering several student versions of the graphic novel based on a solitary excerpt from the book.

Smells Like Teen Shakespeare responds to the teenage approach to life through the rigid structure of the Shakespearean Sonnet.

Pandemic Panic is a collection of writing that addresses the very real stress of what it is like for a teenager when the entire world is turned on its ear by an invisible enemy. Quarantine dreams and stranger things.

Deep Rhetoric shows our writers doing their level best to deploy as many rhetorical modes as possible in poetic form.

Random Haiku brings our twelfth volume of Zuckerbook to a close, with little glimpses into the minds of our students, expressed within the discipline of Haiku.

Enjoy.

Erik J. Hilden
Faculty Advisor,
The Zuckerbook Project.

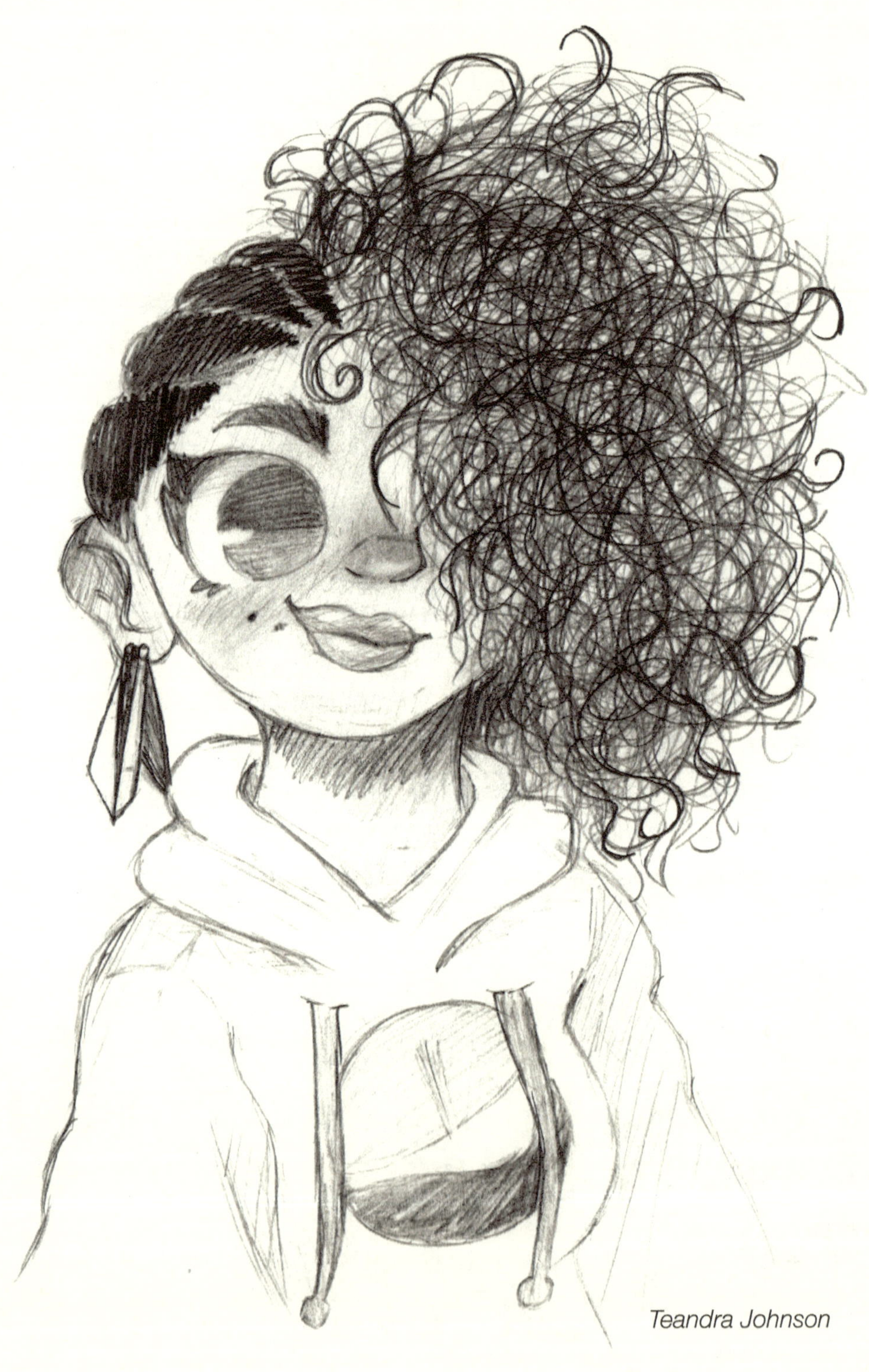

Teandra Johnson

1 Angry Little Birds

Pain and Anger

Christopher Brown

All my life there was pain and angry force to do
What my parents told me.
NO.
I make my decisions.
I'm not your baby anymore;
I will become my own man.

My life is not your life. My life
Is my life. My career is on the line, no more sitting
Around waiting for it to come to me.
NO, I have to care.
After my part, I let everything fall in line.

Teen

Tyreek Chappell

It's the teen's time.
The teen's time.
Nothing ever seems to be right,
So use the pen to write.

I always wondered why we needed feelings.
To see who we are?
To understand life?
No, it's so that we feel alive.

But my feelings are not right.
I feel dead inside.
My mind is going left, so why are you going right?
I and Mind always seem to fight.

Cause she is on my mind
And she is coming from behind.
I rather drop it all, I want to stop it all.
But I can't stop the voice who does it all.

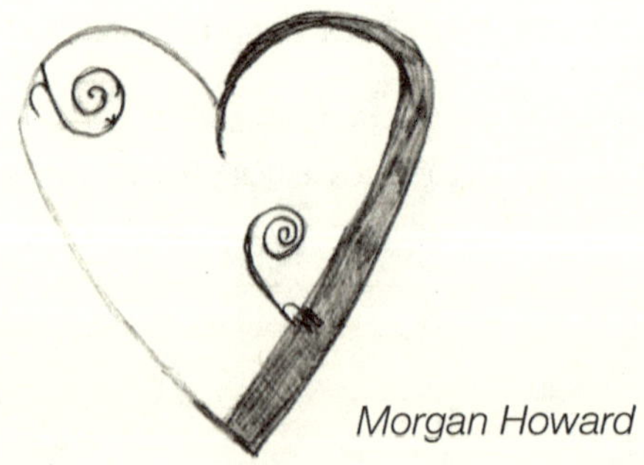

Morgan Howard

Love is Many Things

Neida Hernandez Avila

Love is something that can be sweet and gentle.
But also cold and full of lust.
Even filled with jealousy and insecurities.
Love is something that can be nice
And gentle or dark and cold.

The love you gave me was sweet,
But there were many times I had to reassure you.
So confused; whether you were in love
Or if you were hung up on the last one.

You gave me love,
Or at least you tried.
There were so many things that went wrong,
And many that were right.
The little moments we had were wonderful.

But it all went downhill with just a moment
Where we both went wrong.
Just letting you know,
You were the one I wanted.
Love can be nothing but an illusion.

I Need You

Meagan Brown

I've ruined myself for falling in love.
I continue to go down this broken fork road once again.
Not knowing what the future holds for me.
Taking risks because it's the only thing I trust.

The devil and angel that sit
On my shoulder continue to defeat me.
Being a reflection of myself,
Telling me that I'm in denial.
These voices continue to fight me,
Leaving me vulnerable and hopeless.

I can only ask for you to love me again.
Doing everything you need to
Have you in my arms again.
Despite the bad lingering taste you have,
Will you be able to promise to stop time?

To keep this moment and not let
The future or past ruin us?
Forgetting those mistakes cherishing the
Things that didn't harm us.
Living in the moment with fewer worries.
Only wanting your antidote to
Break me from this heartache.

Moonchild

Spring Lara

Under this sky,
A shining light.
Part of this moonlight.
This moonchild.

No longer in darkness.
Under the moonlight,
Where does this moonchild belong?
Not afraid.

You'll shine.
Your time has come.
Don't cry anymore
In the moonrise.

When the moon rises
You'll shine brighter than ever before.
This is you.
You are the moonchild.

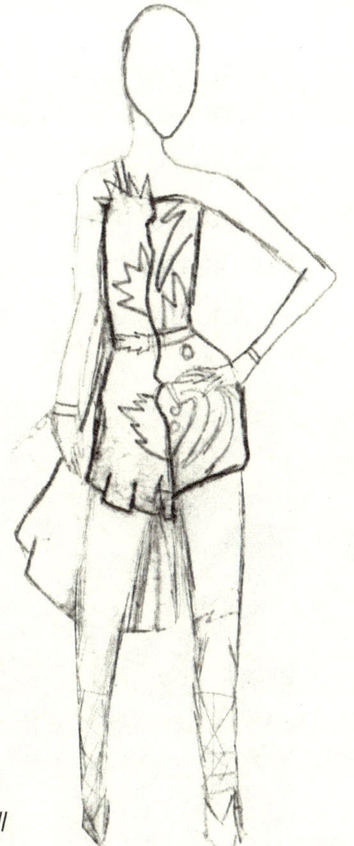

Tanaysha Chappell

Why Did You Come

Kaleelah El-Amin

Why did you come?
Why won't you go?
Where do you arise from?
When can you go?

My family is hurt
Because of you,
And your friends hurt my feelings, too.
Why are you here?

Just to haunt us.
I don't know when you will disappear.
Only you know
Why you come.
But please go in peace
To where you come from.

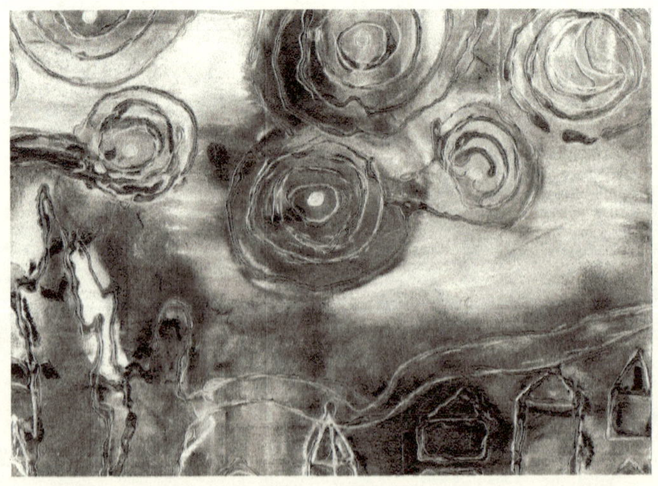

Euphoria

Spring Lara

The feeling
When the sun sets.
A dream,
A beautiful oasis.

Over that horizon
You are there.
So far, but close.
My euphoria.

Wondering,
Staying in endless dreams.
Don't go,
This is the cause of my euphoria.

You are that feeling
Over that horizon.
There is
Euphoria.

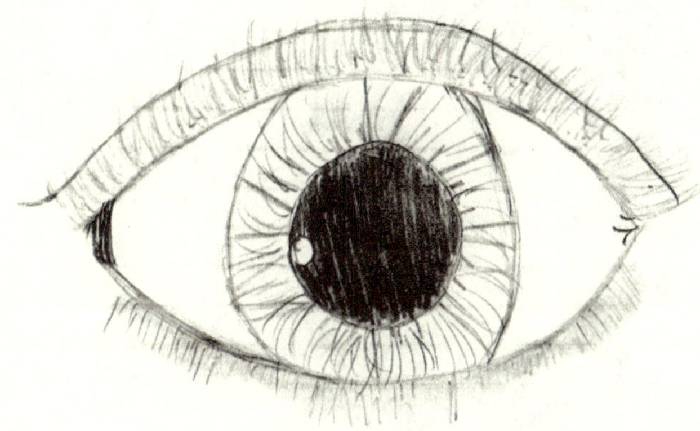

Morgan Howard

What is Love?

Ahmara Richardson

You all claim you know love,
But do you?
Have you felt the warming of another's heart?
Did you feel butterflies in your stomach?

What is love?
Does love make you feel worthless
And make you do things you never imagined?
Being alone is better.

There is no one left to hurt you.
What is love?
Love is something that can be given back,
Then ripped away at any point in time.

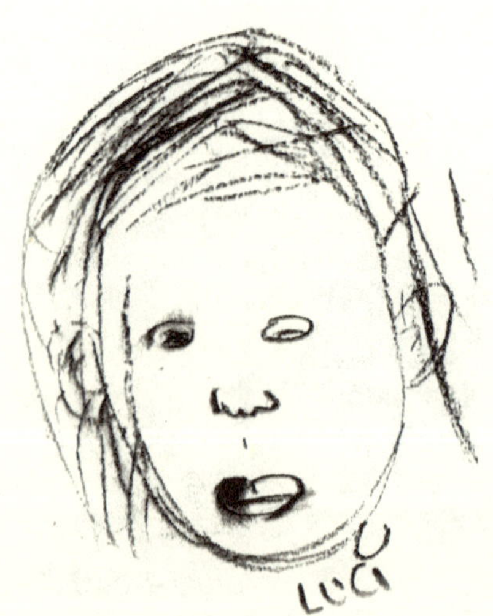

Love is what makes people feel pain,
Something that hurts forever, even if you pretend it doesn't.
What is love?
We all claim we feel love,
But do we?

We let it drive us insane,
Love breaks you down then attempts to put you back together.
It's a heartache.
It is misery.

What is love?
Are any of us even worthy of love?
Are we capable of handling it?
Can we survive the pain?

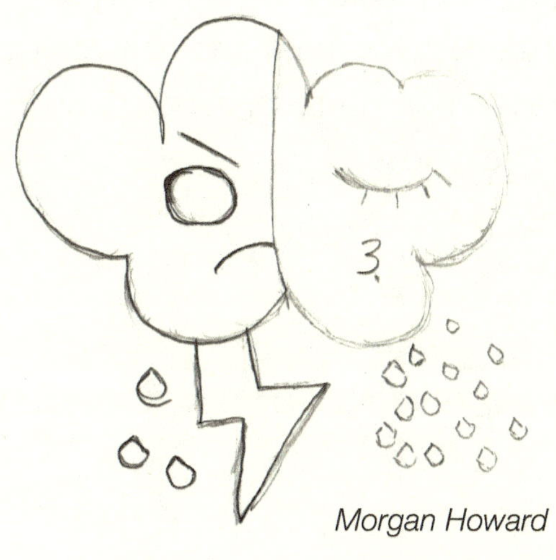

Morgan Howard

Two Yous

Tyreek Chappell

There are two yous.
The sad one, and
The one that is glad.
Which one are you?

Many are happy to be loved.
People who wear masks to protect their faces,
Though they don't protect their hearts.
Only so many people can hold up for so long.

This is to you.
This is from me.
These are my feelings in a bottle
So would you open it for me?
Or it will fill up and burst.

Bursting for you, but breaking because of me.
Since I must hide with my mask and be two of me,
Because there is no one but me, there are two,
And I alone must choose.

Truth Untold

Spring Lara

Full of loneliness,
Sorrow,
Painfully alone,
Withering in a dark castle.

No name
I can say.
This secret, I hold,
Wearing a mask to cover it.

This resembles you,
This special flower.
I can't see you.
I must hide this truth.

I am afraid.
Keep running from this truth.
For all to be thrown away.

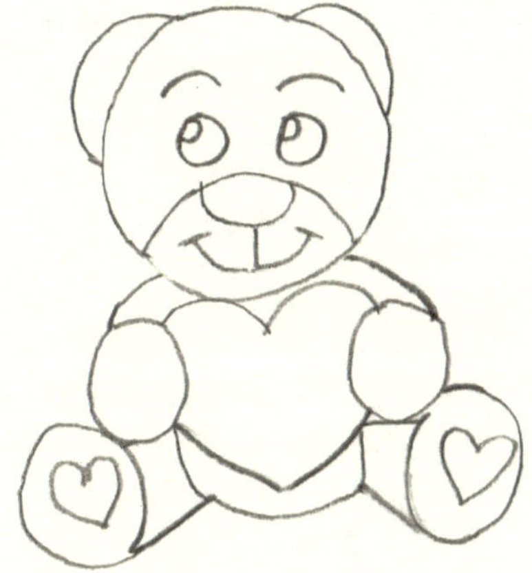

Jaliyah Fair

Lovey-Dovey

Victoria Doctor

Oh, so lovey-dovey.
Oh, so gushy and mushy.
It makes me sick
That people are so mean.

Oh, the love, happiness, and joy
It just brings me annoyance.
The secrets people keep
Make it longer so deep.

Will you be my valentine?
Oh no, I like passion vine.
It makes a girl a creep,
And it makes the boys weep.

Why do people cry
When their hearts do not comply?
It is a dangerous game,
And people always complain.

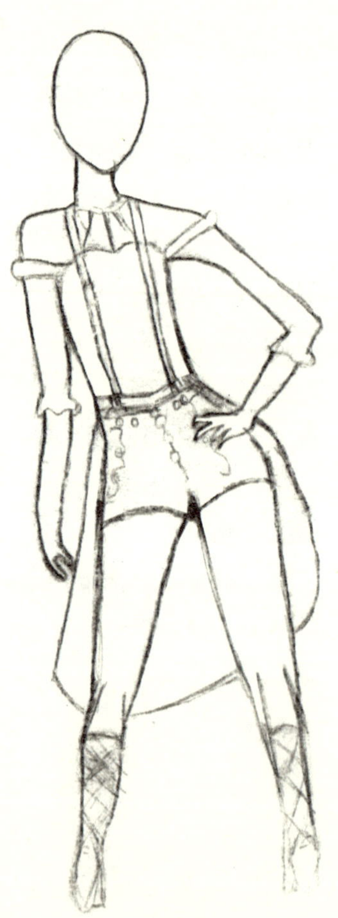

Tanaysha Chappell

I Had To Write A Poem

Elliott Avila

So this day I had to write a poem.
The type of poem I don't know what to write.
The poem of me being an idiot.
I am writing a poem that doesn't have anything
But just me not knowing what to write.

That type of poem that makes you feel
Like you have a stinky brain.
But if I did know what to write in a poem,
I would have a nice looking poem.

While I'm writing this poem of nothing,
I am thinking in my little brain.
What to write in this poem? I can
Only think of a poem with
Nothing in my head.

No rhyming or anything.
I heard a ringtone on a
Hidden overpriced calculator, meaning
I only have a few minutes
To write, to finish the
Poem of nothing.

This is the type of poem of nothing
That has nothing. And it should.

Breakdown

Ahmara Richardson

Breaks you down and makes you cry,
You claim you will always be mine.
Scared you can't fall asleep,
The world has chosen to fill the world with creeps.

Talks to me late at night,
I'm here to hug you and hold you tight.
We get mad and walk away,
I will stay with you until my dying day.

I promise to keep telling you the truth,
With me, there will always be proof.
I would give you the world if I could,
I will love you the way I should.
I have issues and I'm trying my best,
I won't give up so don't protest.

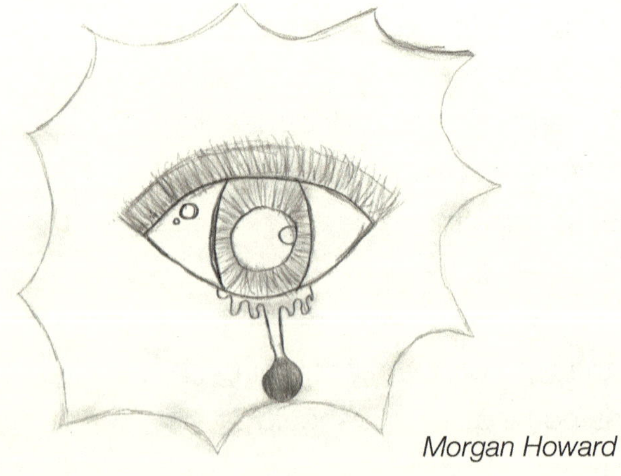

Morgan Howard

Beautiful Darkness

Neidi Rodriguez

Darkness.
I considered darkness
A beautiful thing.
Just imagine
Stepping outside,
Or looking out a window,
Seeing beautiful stars,
And the moon
Brightening your way
As you go.

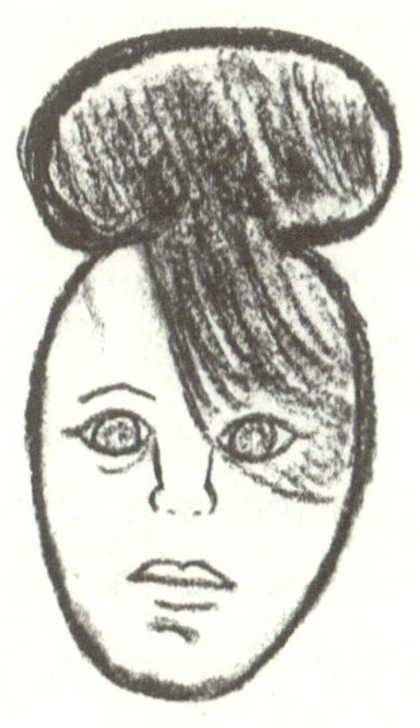

It's just so
Beautiful.

Many think of darkness as
Something sad,
When it is actually
Peaceful.

The moonlight
And stars above
Are peaceful
And calming.
I love the darkness.

Anger and Hate

William Avila Avila

Every day and afternoon I am
Treated with no respect.
My parents are nice and
mean at the same time.
When I do something

Wrong I get yelled at,
And my life is trash.
But I don't get
Yelled at that much.
My mother is a pain in my life; she
Is like the needle hurting me.
My father is so different
From my mother.
He treats me with
Respect and kindness.

My father is my protector.
He helps me, and takes good care of me.
My mother also takes good care of me.
My two sisters are what make my
Mother filled with anger and hate.

Dark Side

Muhammad Bouregba

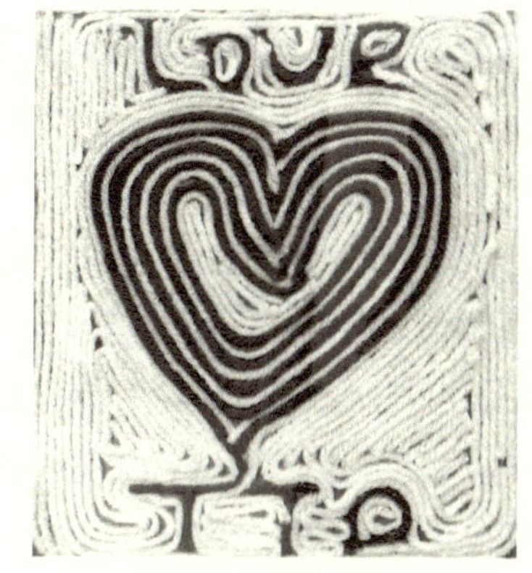

Blood, guts, cuts.
What's more rust to lose?
Life is to gain one more,
I was told.

Life comes in many forms,
Like an apple.
So many, all different kinds,
But there is a bad apple in the bunch.

Everyone has a dark side.
Some don't show it, but I do.
I'm like a shadow,
Always behind something.

I feel the venom in my blood.
This world will see what comes.
There is a new evil coming,
And I'm not like the Joker or anything.

The real deal is
Who doesn't yield
Is here.
It's my dark side.

What Comes with Every Fire?

Jamya Washington

Each sinner has a soul, and
Every soul has a sinner.
Every birth there's a death.
He took a match and created fire,
"What is fire?" he asked himself.
But then he realized there's
No one to turn to.
"Why keep breathing when you're
Close to death? Don't stop now!" he said.
What comes with every fire? Death?

He met a girl... who was once
Very special to him,
But his match burned out.
And she was no longer special.
She figured out that
She wasn't meant to be,
So she moved on.

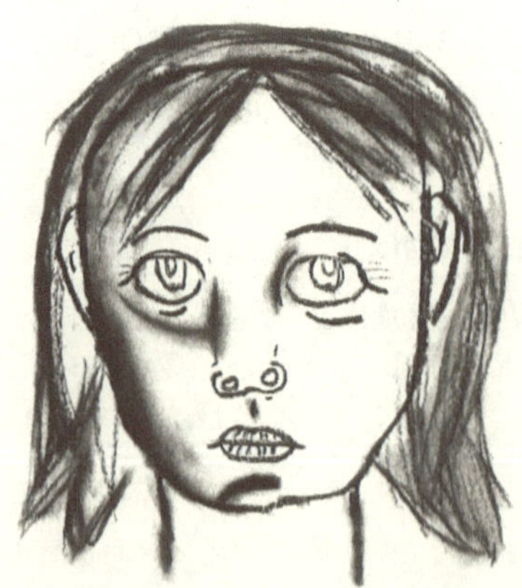

But then he realized his
Soul was sinning without her.
He hurt, blamed and
Disowned his parents.
What comes with every fire? Death?

He lit the match one last time,
Looking for a spark.
He accidentally dropped the match,
Lighting the floor on fire.
It went from the bed to the walls.
He moved closer to the
Window and fell.
Holding on for dear life,
And he saw the girl as
She walked past,
Waiting for his death.
And he finally let go…
What comes with every fire? Death?

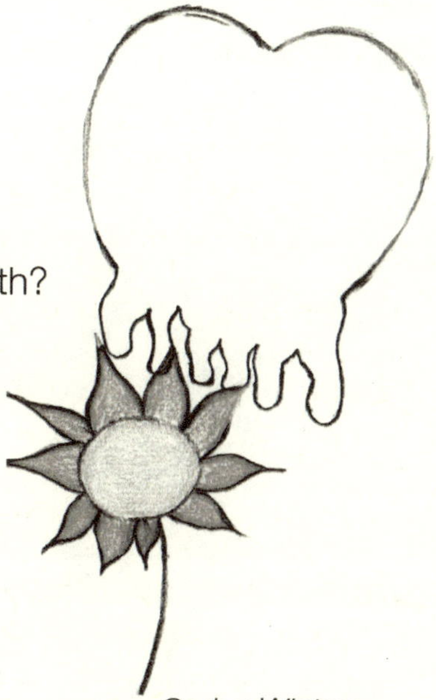

Caden Winters

They Broke It

Hoody Alverez

I can't love it anymore.
I can't get lost in the music.
Not anymore.
I can't play the saxophone.
It becomes lost,
Because…
They broke it.

I can't drown out the sounds
Of twisted minds
Because they broke it.

I can't,
Because
They broke it.

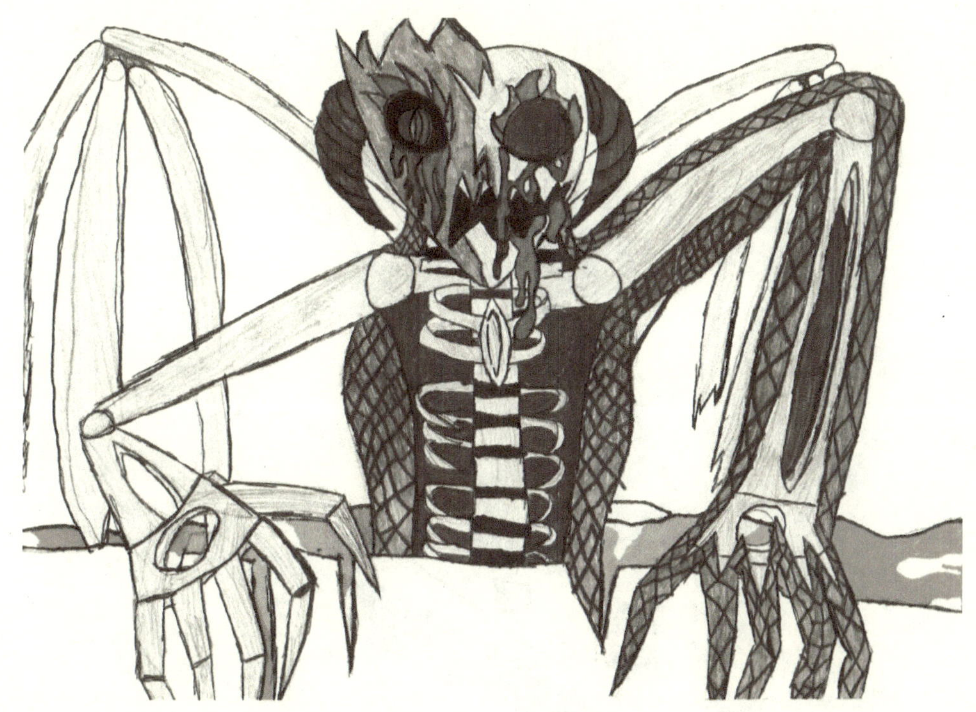

Nathan Juarez

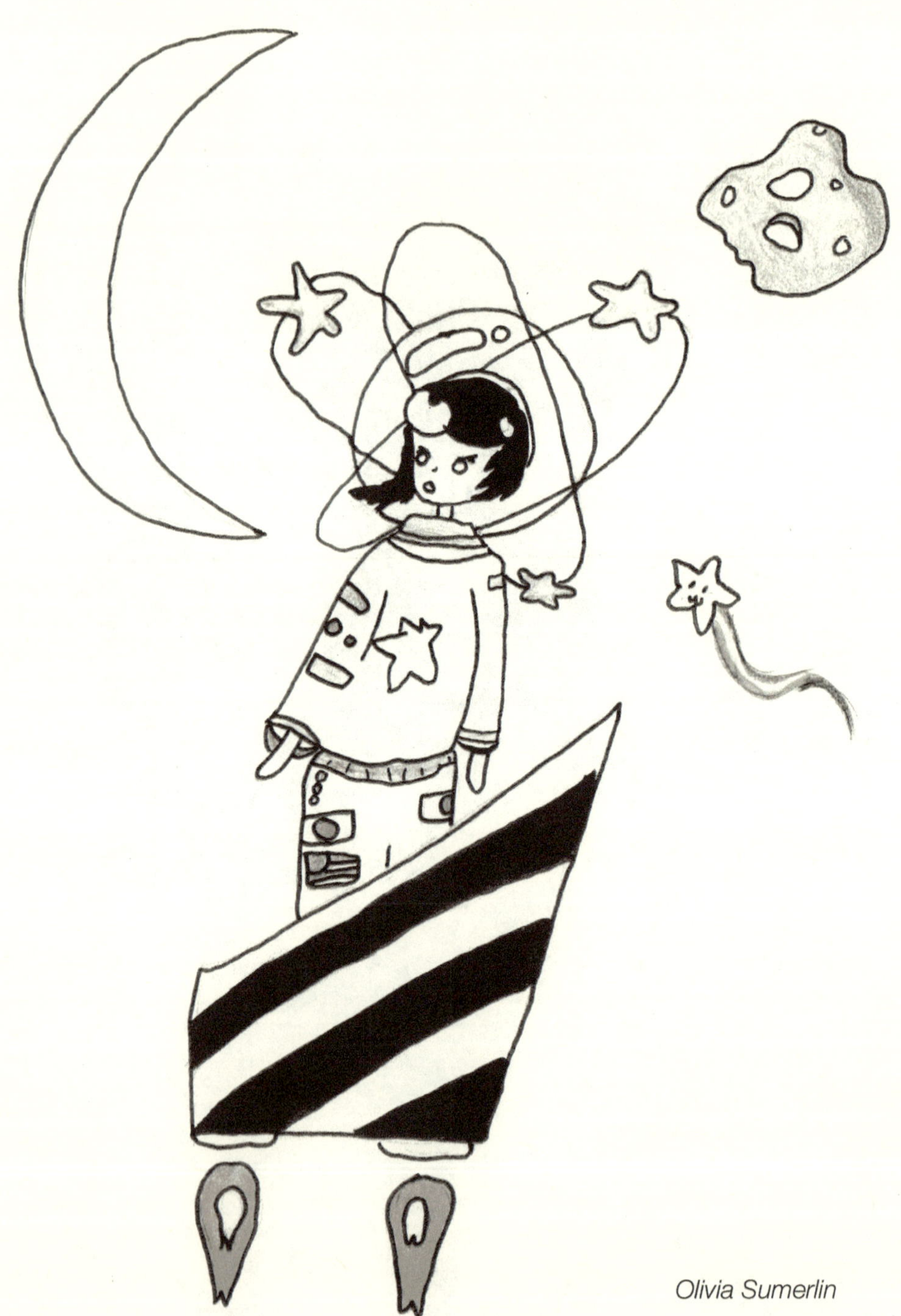

Olivia Sumerlin

2 No Guard Rail

The Two Rabbits

Muhammad Bouregba

The two rabbits jumped as high as the clouds
As they fought against the red bird of flames.
The rabbits were Yin and Yang, and
The bird was the Vermilion Bird, the symbol of fire.

They fought for five weeks until the Qilin
Came from the dust and stopped the fighting.
The good came back as the bird flew
To its cave in the fiery mountains.

The rabbits jumped upon the back of the Qilin
And rode him back to the light and dark.

I Used to be Me

Teandra Johnson

I used to be me,
But now I am someone else,
Because I can't be me if I
Don't know who I am.

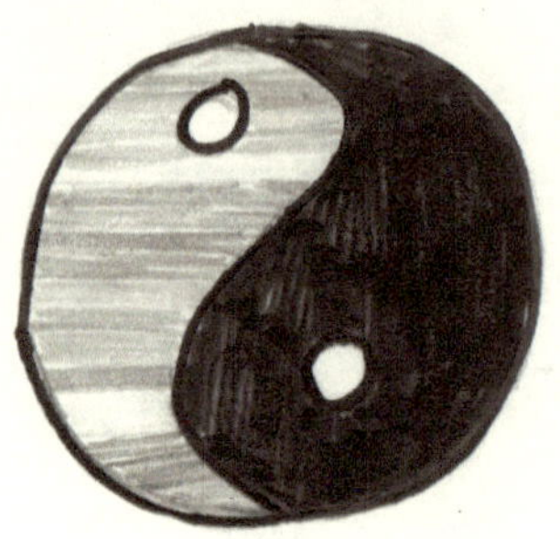

Morgan Howard

I am lost and confused.
I wonder what I used to be.
I hear hate words piling up.
I see them cover me like a sheet.
I want to be found
In this covering.
I am lost and confused.

I pretend I am them.
I feel trapped in these chains.
I touch the steel bars.
I worry I won't find myself.
I cry for happiness.
I am lost and confused.

I understand that reality is hidden.
I say what is true to me.
I dream they will notice the fakeness.
I try to survive the useless judgment.
I hope we switch places soon.
I am lost and confused.

During the Night

Priceless Johnson

In my day, I crave to be asleep, dreaming of you.
I wish to be having joyous
Dreams, and let my imagination run free.
The clock ticks slower on those days.

I most need it not to be
"O Romeo, Romeo! Wherefore art
Thou Romeo? Come save me, my
Love...from my weakness and hopelessness!"

A delivering fairy godmother will reward
Me with shoes and more. I'll dance the
Night away with you but unintentionally
Leave a glass slipper. The dream will end with a

Happily ever after.
My dreams filled with you
Make it worth it all. Be the one
For me and stay in my dreams.

Viva La Revolution

Victoria Doctor

Here we fight.
Hear the cries of terror from us.
But no, we are considered treasonous.
We are excluded, withtheir backs turned.

It all makes my stomach churn.
I see them with their stony stares,
But we will soon settle our affairs.
Look at me and laugh with your prideful dares.

All they will soon see is a flare.
We shall fight and rise soon to commence.
Why do these people have to be so dense?
We plan for battle as we go to fight.

This time we will definitely use all our might.
We have to fight for ourselves and back.
Oh, how much I want to give them a smack.
I will very soon find a solution.

And so I say to you,
"Viva La The Revolution!"

Let's Start A Revolution

Brooklynn Martin

Let's start a revolution and kill each other.
We might as well die.
It's going to happen one day.

Let's start a revolution and make it all end.
Start a new life.
Bring peace to our land.

Let's start a revolution, make us equal.
Women can do the same
As can men do the same.

Let's start a revolution; all hail the President.
Let's get him now,
Before he makes America worse again.

Let's start a revolution; get everyone in.
Spread it around
Bring all of your friends.

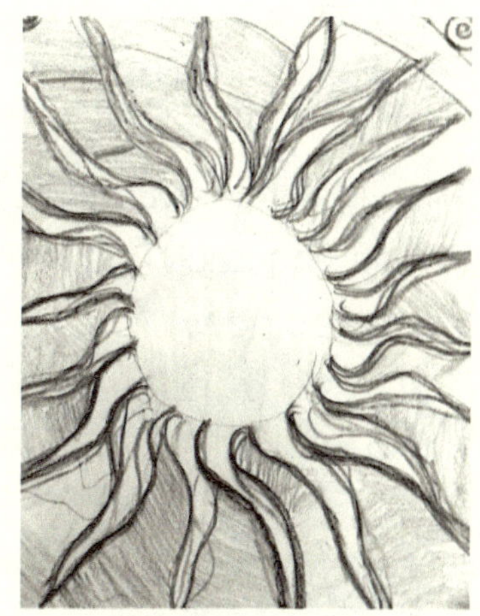

Jealousy

Maniyah Yates

Why is that we're still being punished
When we shouldn't?
For something that we became free of years ago?
Some people can't leave the past alone.

Now that we're on your level, it's a problem?
That's not how it works, for starters.
We've gotten beaten, hung, and shot.
For what?

For trying to escape from the torture?
Of being the color, you're not?
We've planted crops.
We've cleaned your houses.

We've taken care of your children.
We've cooked your FOOD!
Now that we try to do the same for us,
We still get punished.

That time was over years ago.
Please bag back and let it go,
We're free now,
And minding our own business.

Owning our own expensive cars, houses and
Going to the best schools is a problem.
Y'all think we can't do things for ourselves.
We want to buy something expensive.

Show you the money.
You start asking questions, probably thinking,
"How'd they get this money, probably stole it."
Then start asking more questions.

Y'all minds are so stuck far in the past.
I guess it's too hard to believe
That money came from HARD
WORK and DEDICATION!

The cycle will continue for
As long as this world will last.
I hope one-day people can
Get their heads out of the past.

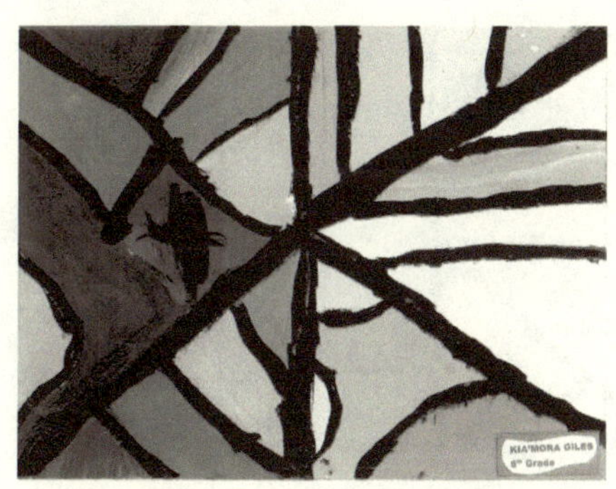

Work to Fight

Victoria Doctor

Our revolution isn't going to slack.
Because our revolution will be whack.
We have to work to fight.
Then we will get more might.

It shall be no play on this very day.
We will be the ones who cry out, "Yay!"
Our revolution shall show no signs of stopping.
Just hope the adults like a whole year of chopping.

Our revolution shall be severe.
I hope everyone isn't too delirious.
I hope everyone is ready for this type of war.
Because this is just the beginning of more.

My revolution shall be all over the world in a second.
I shall not be reckoned or beckoned.
Everything shall soon fall into place.
We shall no longer be a waste of space.

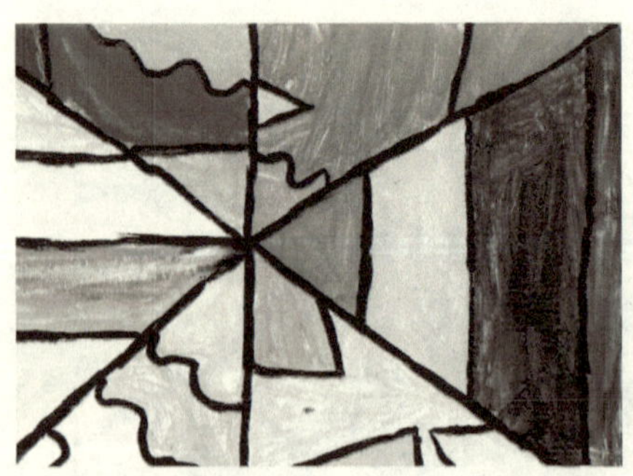

Confusion

Maniyah Yates

We have the right to speak what we want.
We have the right to do what we want.
We have the right to do whatever.
I thought these rights were going to last forever?

The Bill of rights.
The 1st Amendment.
The Constitution.
We obviously have limits...

Why confuse us of thinking we can
Do this and that when we can't?
That just makes our lives harder.
More challenging to maintain.
And it is complicated for us to go farther.

It'll be best just to have us have limits.
Rather than to arrest and punish us for
Something we THOUGHT we could've done.
It's not our fault these new rules and
Limits weren't finalized.
Because if they were, we citizens wouldn't be
Making these everyday mistakes now, would we?

We Cry

Santi Gilliard

We cry, we laugh,
But we keep moving forward.
We keep moving through the harsh words.

We keep moving through the pain given by people
Who is hurting who?
We study, we practice, but yet we are not perfect.

Nobody is perfect, but yet we try to be.
We try to perfect people that are different.
Try to make them feel less than.

Lift people up instead of pulling them down.
Help them when they need it; don't judge them.
Just be kind, and don't be a punk.

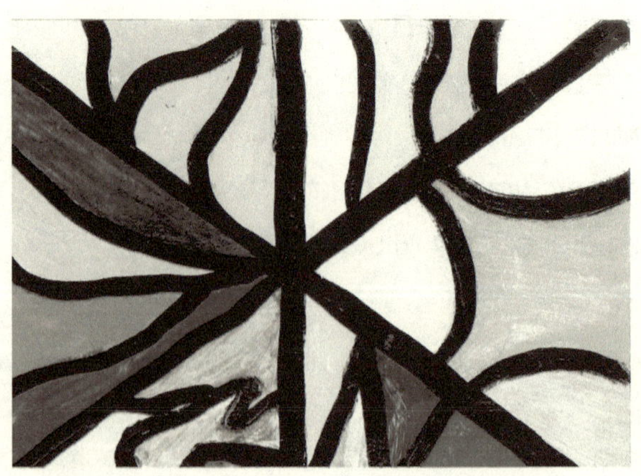

You've Shown Me

Spring Lara

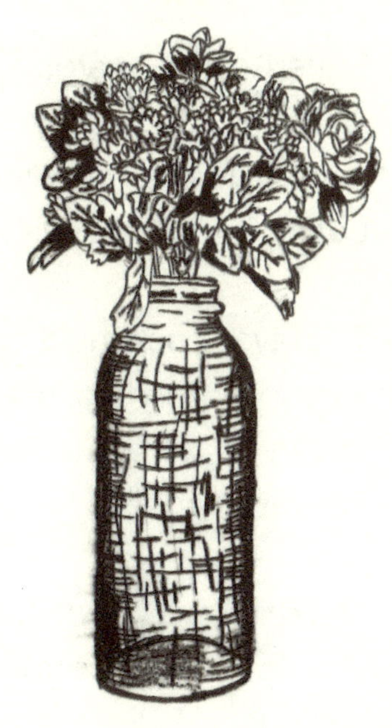

You've shown me
I have the reasons,
Opening my eyes in the dark
Little by little.

The gaze of a cold night,
The target of countless arrows
In frightened eyes.
The only way.

Warfare and pain
Putting back broken glass.
Nothing but a reflection of it
Scattered, irreparable.

Fixing…different.
My surroundings are becoming
More and more transparent.
A sea of many obstacles
To reach the light.

The Rise of a Water Lily

Ameerah King

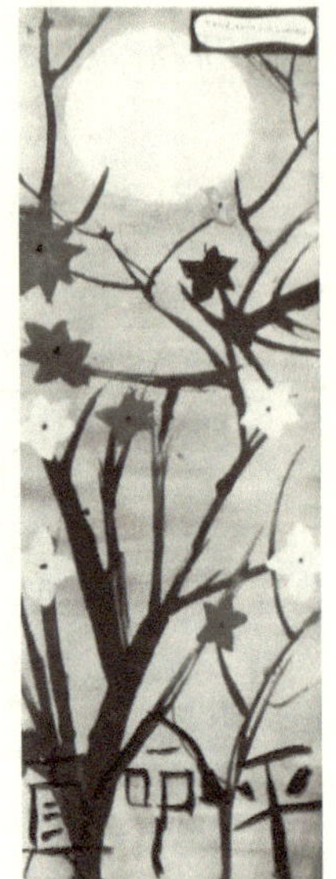

Butterflies flutter around an ethereal abyss.
A dove is intrigued by their purity.
It wants to fly away with them,
But its lifelong acquaintance,

The raven has a hold on him.
The dove didn't accept the raven by choice,
The raven is intrigued by the dove.
The raven goes to lay food for the dove.

The dove gives in despite hesitation.
The dove dreams about different approaches to the Island of Glass.
Sharp edges of glass could potentially kill him.
He welcomes the feelings with opened wings.

Every day the dove goes to the flower bud to help it grow.
The flower is destined to be a beautiful one.
The dove claims the flower as its own
To cherish and protect.
The raven tries to come and pick
The flower piece by piece every day.

He never succeeds.
The flower is always guarded by the majestic butterflies.
The dove has developed a bond with the butterflies.
They guide him.

The raven no longer has its claws
Lodged deep within the dove.
Butterflies annoy him.
The dove, the flower, and the butterflies
Are now tethered together.
The dove still often thinks of the Island of Glass.

The butterflies flutter around him.
The flower has blossomed into a beautiful abstract.
The dove is very proud.
The raven has laid low for a while.

The dove is skeptical but remains peaceful.
All is good and well until a day that is too quiet comes around.
The dove is nowhere to be seen.
The raven is still prowling around, a poisonous insect.

The butterflies aren't fluttering.
The flower is a little dim today.
Days pass, and the dove never returns.
The dove has perished into the Island of Glass.

Somewhere in the ethereal abyss,
A water lily is reborn to leave the dove's message.

The Insulation of Earth

Anastazia Mendones

The breath of winter has yet to dissipate,
Yet an immaculate warmth has spread.
The grass has grown and flowers have
Bloomed to show the beauty of Earth.
A beauty that is much obliged and accepted.
A chance for reincarnation has presented itself,
A chance we have no means to take.

As the rain flows our sins grow as
We stand apart from the rest.
We ran from the water,
A concept needed for survival.
Though the air should be cleaner,
It is still tainted.
Though there should be more trees,
They have been prompted to
A pointless, untimely death.

We yearn for the presence of the sun,
Yet we seek protection when it visits.
We yearn for water
Yet we create a barrier against it.
We yearn for the beauty of nature,
Yet we purge it at any given consent.
We yearn for the innocence
That has long been out of reach.

Spring is the protection
Between cold and heat;
An invention we have acknowledged,
Yet have no pretense of.
We adorn the fictitious coats
That replaces the real thing.
Spring is in the air, yet we can't
See or breathe it into recognition.

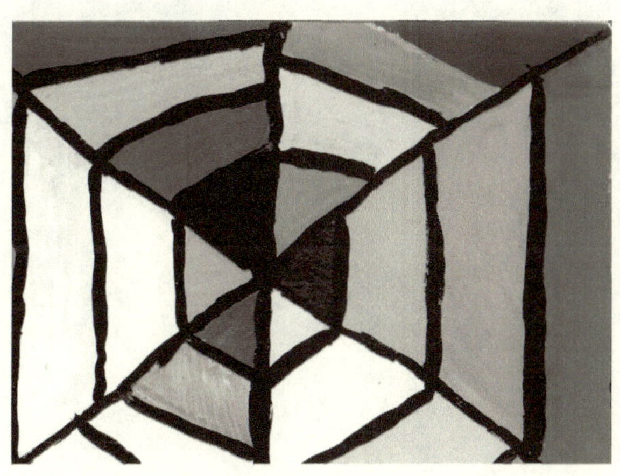

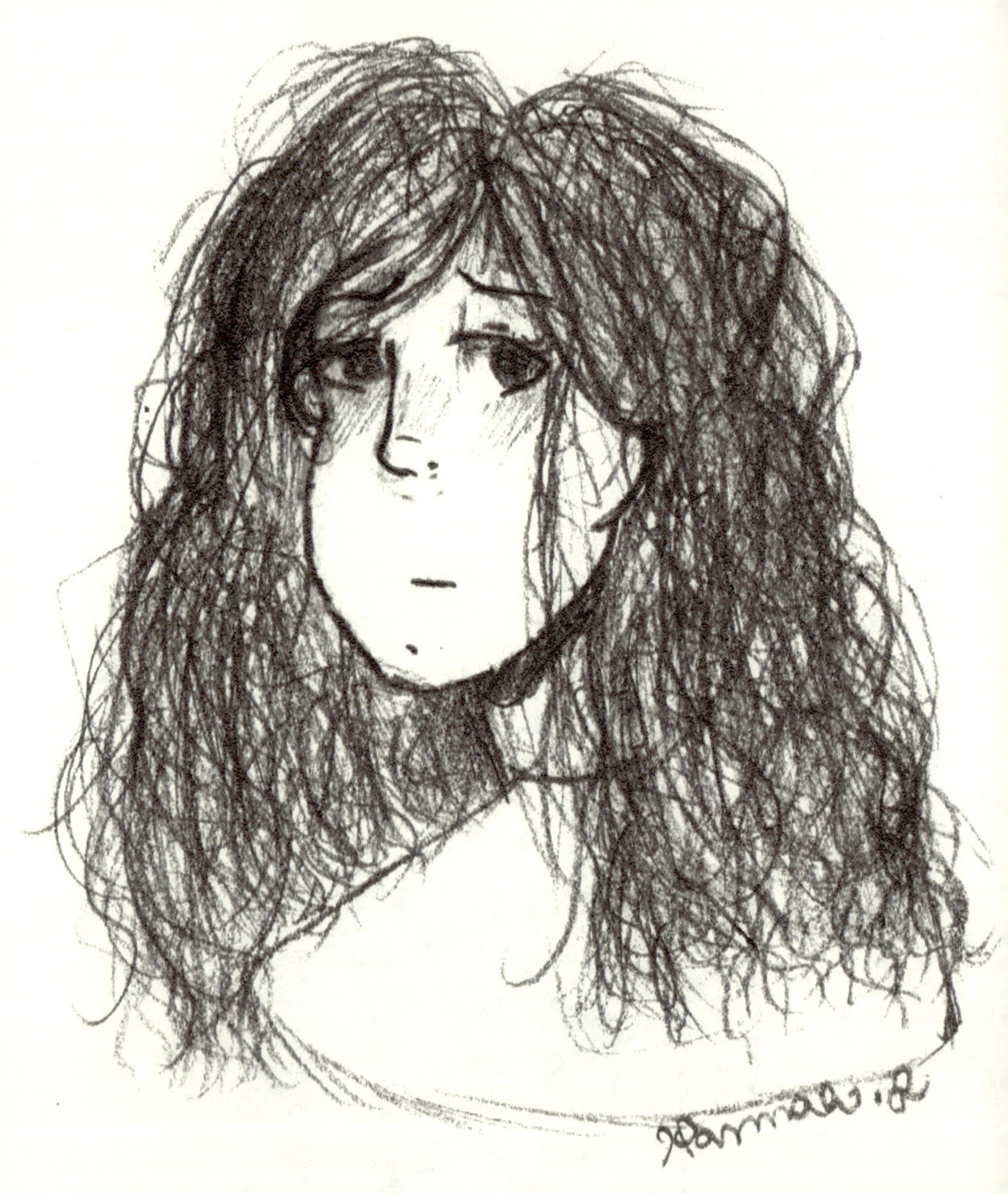

Hannah Jones

3 Mysterious Equation

My Axis Biting Nightmare

Walter Timer

I feel obtuse. Acute. Equilateral.
Parallel but never perpendicular,
A point on a line is neither. My
Trapezoids hurt. A lot. A plot that is
Scattered and shattered in fractals
Fractured in a Mandelbrot cry for

Help. Imaginary and Theoretical.
Another absolute zero.
Cross me. Please. Points on a
Linear plane of existence.
Just try to plot that line of existential being.
Yeah. Just try.

X my Y and Y my Z and what comes after
That? Another plane, another dimension.
My Axis Biting Nightmare.

Me-You=X

Victor Santamaria

Here's an equation you can't solve.
Me-You= X
An equation with a lot of meaning,
With a variable that has a dark side.

A nightmare that'll never end.
But you can solve that problem
Though, at least I can.
Me + You= Infinity

It's beautiful, at least to me.
Like a happy story with no end.
An adventure with new treasures
That hasn't been discovered yet.
A risk that only you and I will take...solve it.

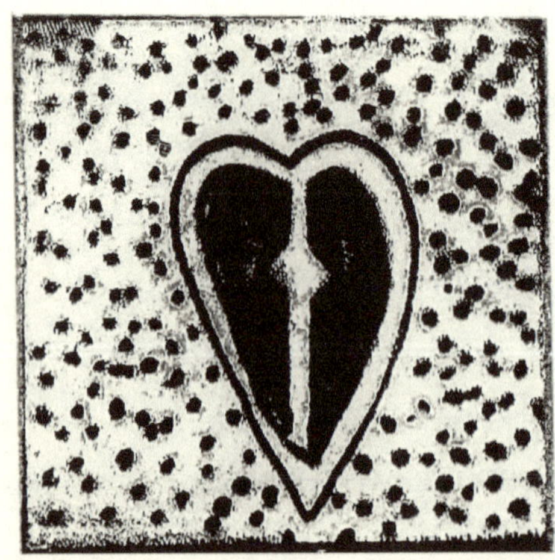

I Want to Add

Emory Rose

I want you to be added into
My life, but never subtracted.

I am trying to focus, but I
Get distracted. I pray to

God that we never ever
Multiply.

My Other Half

Tanaysha Chappell

My love for you is half of the whole
But you're the missing piece.
You add to love and yet you
Make me even more complete.

My love for you is more than
Pi. The numbers don't repeat.
If only you were undefined.
Maybe you could be with me.

Equations

Bradley Perez

He plus he equals love.
Her plus her is the same.
What if that's not it?
Maybe not he or she.

Maybe a variable.
Awaiting to be found.
Wanting to be apart of the equation,
Wanting to find out.

The equation they fit into.
Maybe they fit into every equation,
The one applies to all,

Or the one that applies to none.
Whichever it is,
It'll always start with love.

Solve my Sorrow

Jacob Laycock

Most people are perpendicular,
Always come across each other,
But I'm parallel,
Never going to meet someone.

Love is like the Pythagorean theorem.
No one can solve it,
Except those who are lucky enough
To have a cheat sheet.

I'm like a square,
Shaped at the edges and smooth on the sides.
I'm involved with a lot of problems.
Mostly ones that can't be solved.

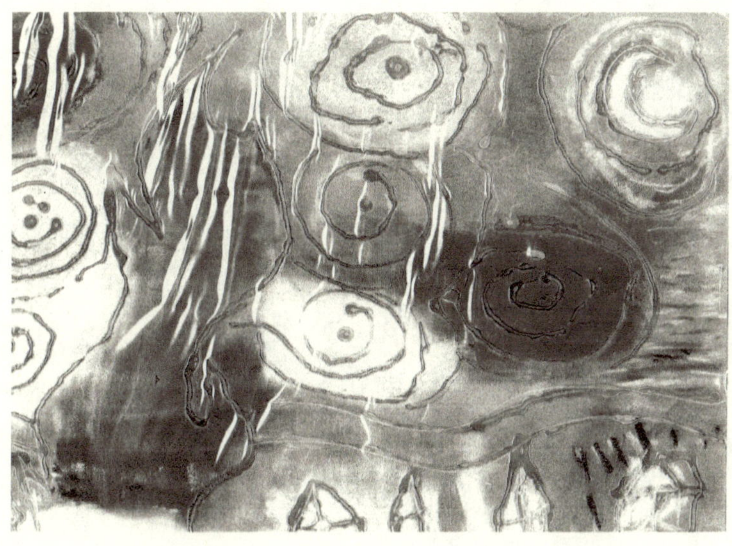

You and I Equals Us

Andrea Ramirez

If you and I add one and one,
That makes two. You are here
For me and I'm there for you.
I just hope that we never subtract one.

Is there any way that our love
It can be like pi? Can we be
Never-ending or are you thinking
Differently? Do you want to be a

Negative or positive slope?
Because I know for a fact
That we can't be undefined.

Slope-Intercept Love

Jah'Sean Brown

I am the slope.
You are my intercept.
You tell me where to start.
You help me find the point.

Without you, I am lost.
Where on the line do I start?
You are the parameter I never want to change.
You are the center of our line that never ends.

Everything

Alajah Thompson

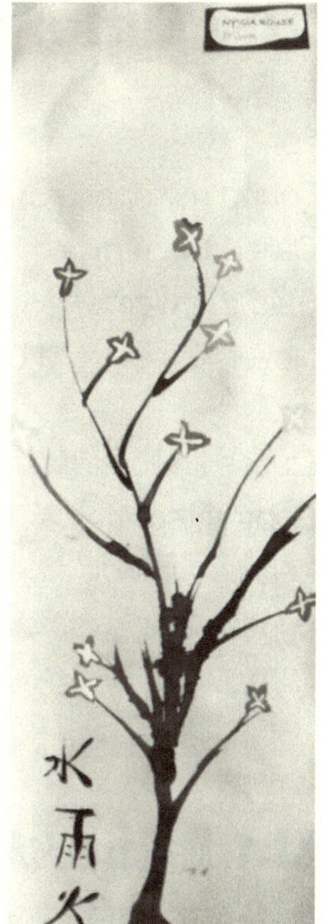

You are an acute person.
You change my rate.
You are an angle.
You make me hotter than 90 degrees.

You complete the empty space
For my perimeter.
I am really at the point
Where you meet my axis.

Blah Blah Blah

Trawley Harper

We are perpendicular,
We are so close but never cross paths.
Is it because we're negative?

It can't be, because I'm positive.
Our lines will never end.
Wait, are we parabola?
Because we seemed to turn around.
No, because the point makes our love bound.

The Difference

Bradley Perez

Found my one in one hundred.
Called them mine,
Said the words.
Never knew you'd be a mean one.

Guess I'm out of range.
Subtracted me,
Learned the difference.
I guess this was never meant to be.

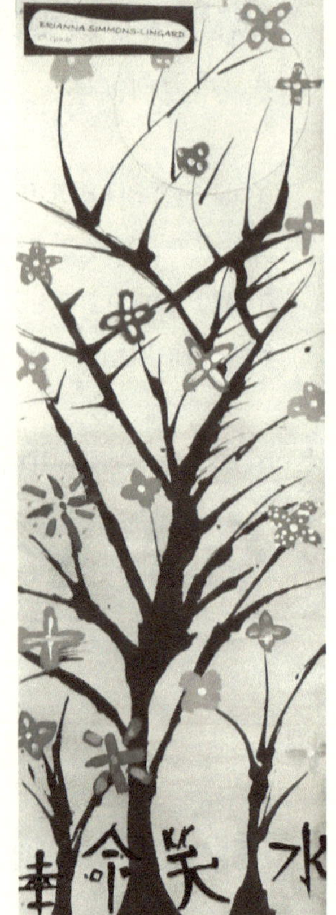

Undefined Love

Diana Gonzales

My love for you is undefined.
You make me horizontal.
You complete the other half to my heart.

My love for you is like an oval.
I think I've won a Nobel Prize.
You complete the equation.
That gets rid of my temptation.
You're like the pi to my circumference.

Cupid Failed

Jackie Velasquez

Destiny coordinated us to be together.
If it weren't for cupid failing again,
We'd be like perpendicular lines.
Sadly, we're like parallel lines.
Same distance but
We
Never
Cross.

Drugs Like Love

Joshua Hernandez

Love is like a drug.
You don't understand it.
But you keep on wanting
It. It is an addiction.

You keep on wanting to
Do it but don't want
To move on.

Fractions

Alma Trejo

Two fractions unite
And become a whole number
And form a constant bond of love,

Showing our common differences.
As the power of our love grows solid.
And ignites a fire.

One More

Deysi Monzon

Uno mas uno san
Dos ojitos para ver la gran
Belleza que lleuas.
Para ti los "step equations
Son difíciles y para mi es dificil de poder
Tener tu amor.

Vez que para poder resolver
Un absolute value tienes
Que cambiar los números.

Y muertos yo no te
Cambiaria por nadie
Y si te mueves me
Nuevo Contigo.

Adding

Damion Brown

I was up to no good.
I had too many girls.
At my school, I had 3.

At my reading camp, I have 2,
And 4 that live by me.
6 that don't live in my state

And 5 at my old school.
There's no way I can have 16 girls.
Something I don't know now.

I'm gonna do this.

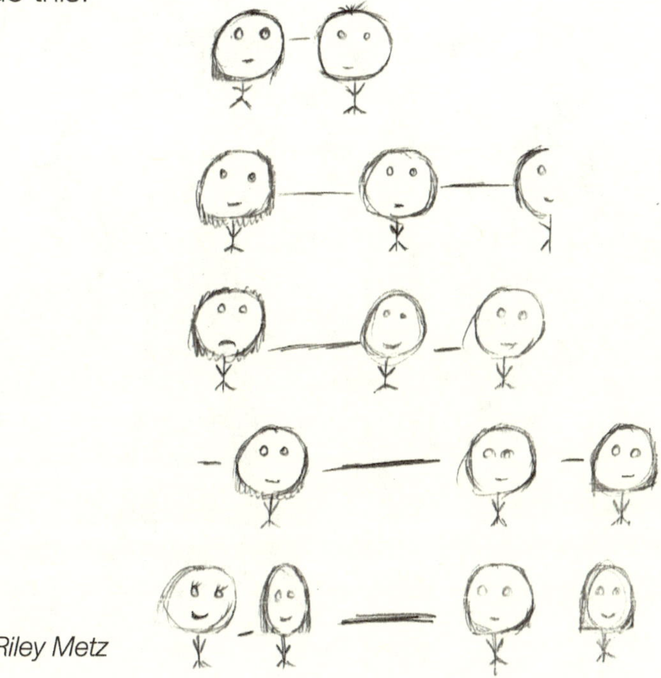

Riley Metz

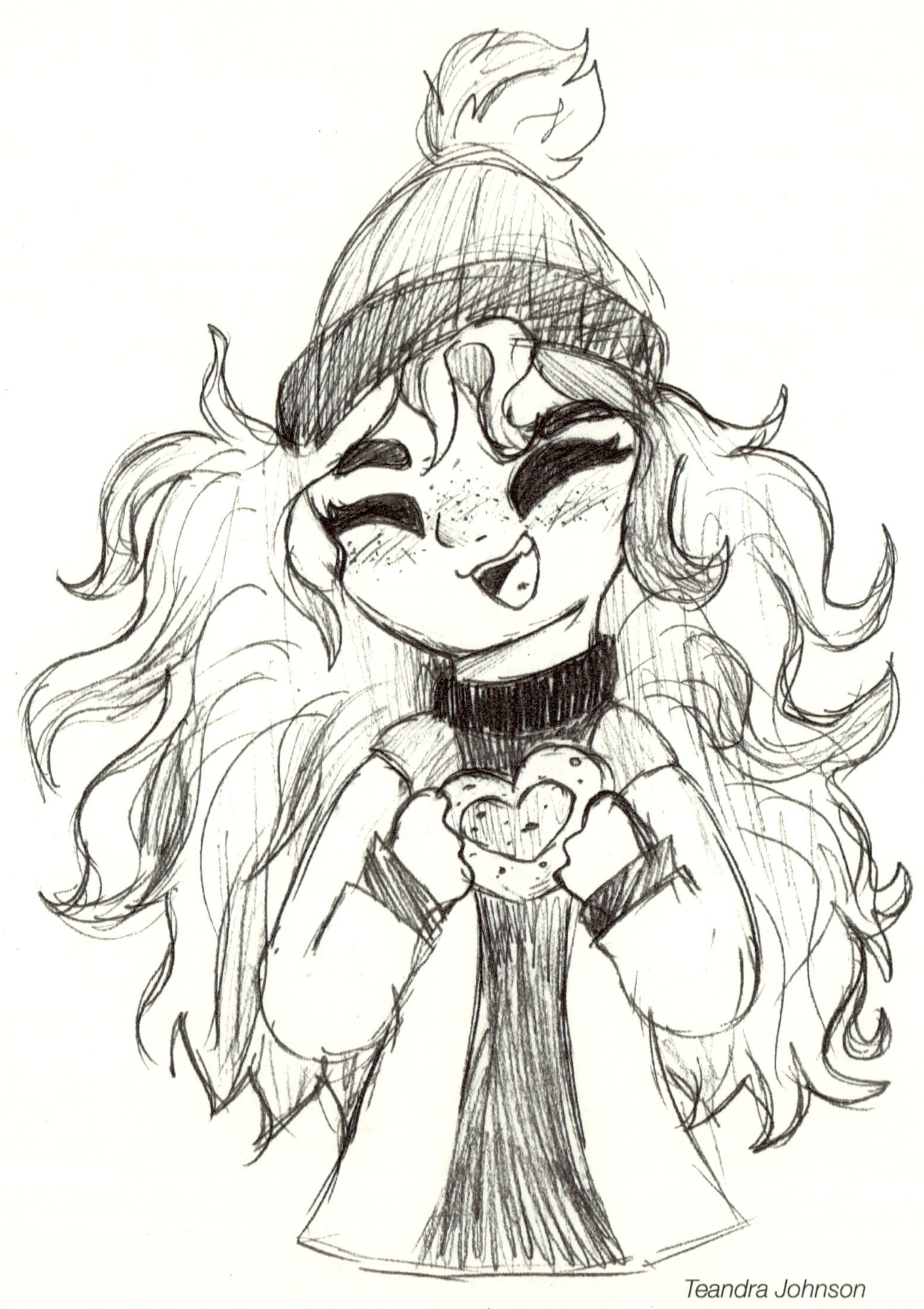

Teandra Johnson

4 Chemically Speaking

Chemistry

Shekynah Moore

I wish I knew more about chemistry
So I could have a you
And me,
Though our mix is dangerous.

I don't care as long as
You are with me.
But you're too fly.
You're breaking gravity.
You're floating away from me.

Love in The Laboratory

Devery Howard

Chemistry: The complete emotional
Or psychological interaction between
Two people.
We have chemistry,
You and me. You are my ATP.
You supply my energy.

Like the process of cellular
Respiration, you keep me alive.
You are the independent variable
Of my experiment. You affect me.

Spark Electricity

Ja'Lea Anderson

We spark electricity; you are
What matters to me.
I have a hypothesis:
You belong with me,
Like oxygen is needed to breathe.

The weather changes every day, but not
Like my feelings for you.
It would be out of control.
My feelings for you are like
A volcano that is about to explode.

The Salty Tears of Science

Shekynah Moore

Every blue moon, you want me
To be there.
Every phase of your life I will
Be there.

Even though you don't want
Me too.
I'll cry salty tears of science.

Every time you leave,
I love you.
But you don't love me.

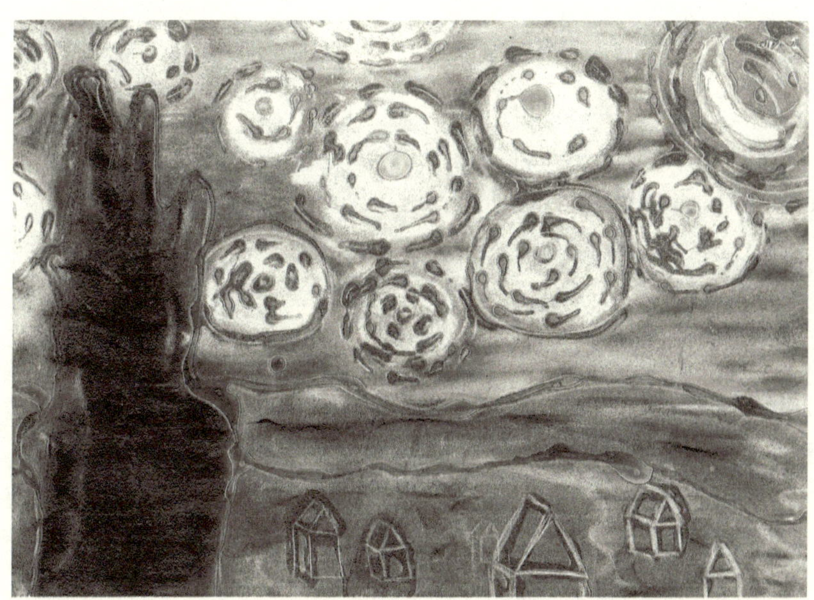

What's Behind the Chemistry?

Riley Metz

The chemistry behind us is strong.
You make my heart do a 360° degree spin.
I wish I could be around you 24/7.
My temperature reaches 451° when I am with you.

If you were an angle, you'd be acute.
You make my heart explode like a block of TNT.
You're the radius or diameter,
But together we make a whole.
You make my heart explode like Mentos in Coke.

I'm Trying to Remain Whole

Shekynah Moore

You've been divided from me.
You've been my everything.
The chemistry between us has
Faded into a negative.

All variables around you
Distract you.
You've left me alone.
I guess you're not my chromosome.

I Internally Feel Chemicals!

Andrea Ramirez

Why can I internally feel chemicals?
Yeah, I get it; chemicals are for science.
But who knew you could feel it inside and out?
If you get sizzles, what do they mean?

Have I consumed chemicals, or am I daydreaming?
Sizzles aren't normal for me.
Why do I feel them? I might have consumed chemicals,
Or am I in love?

The sizzles won't stop because my
Love for you can't stop.
The chemicals are making you crazy?
It's like they are all trapped inside.

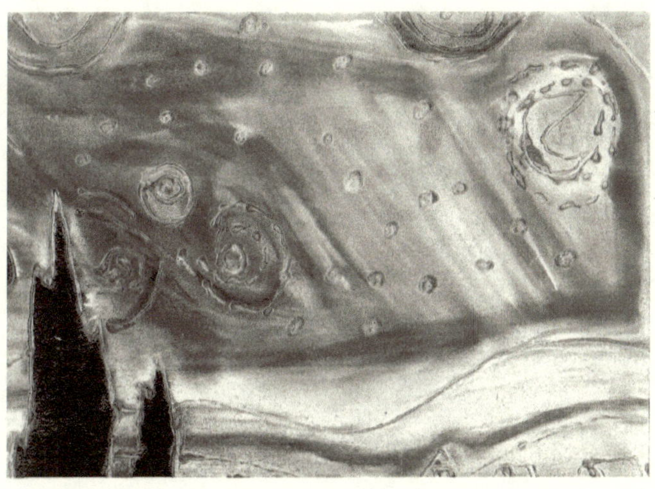

Acid Love

Bradley Perez

Thought that it was love
But chemistry existed not.
Found an antidote.
But your response was poison.

Like water added to the acid,
A mess as a result.
Broken and shattered.

The toxicity is deadly.
I shouldn't be with you,
Yet the poles somehow attract.

Messed with my brain.
Messed with my heart.
Now it's a blur,
Like fog caused by vapor.

Now I'm here,
Drowned in a pool of toxins.
Forever hurt
And forever scarred.

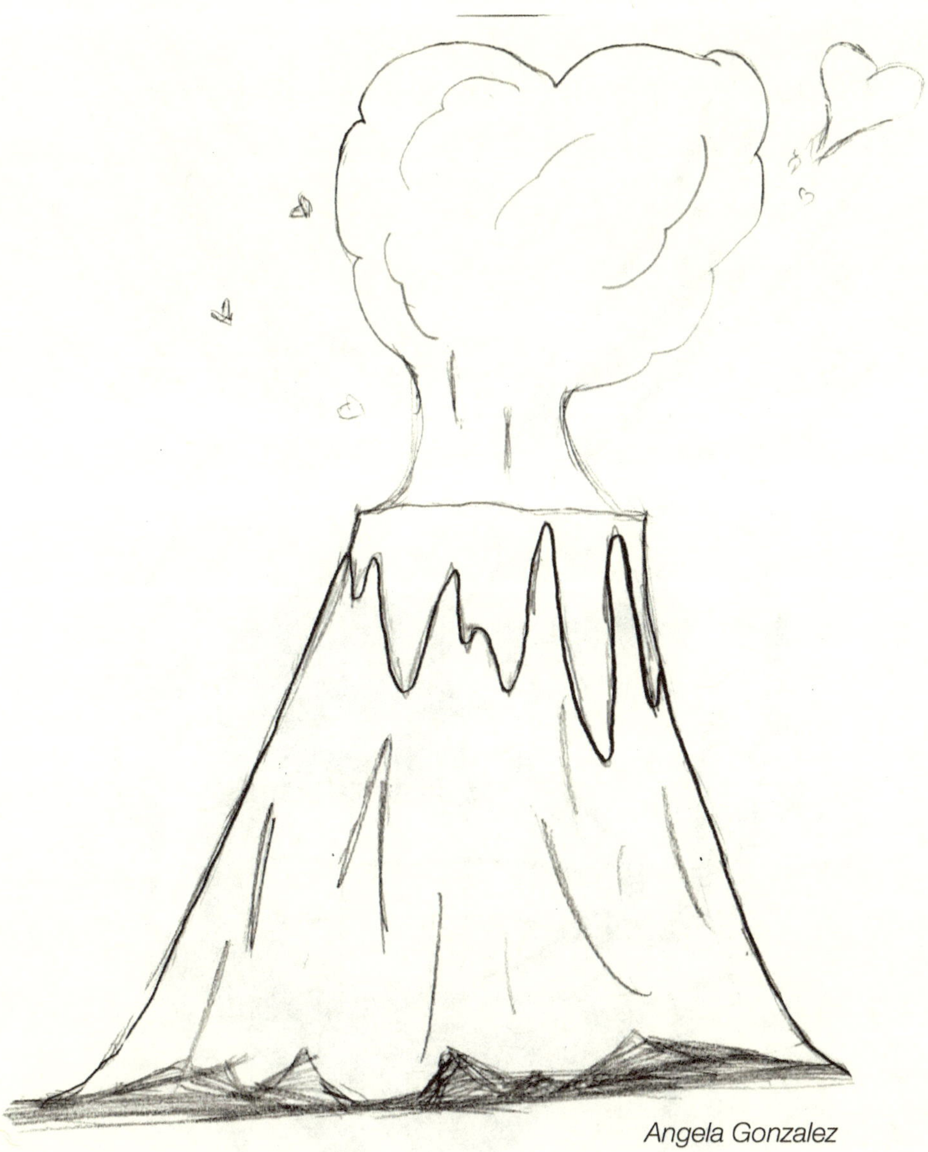

Angela Gonzalez

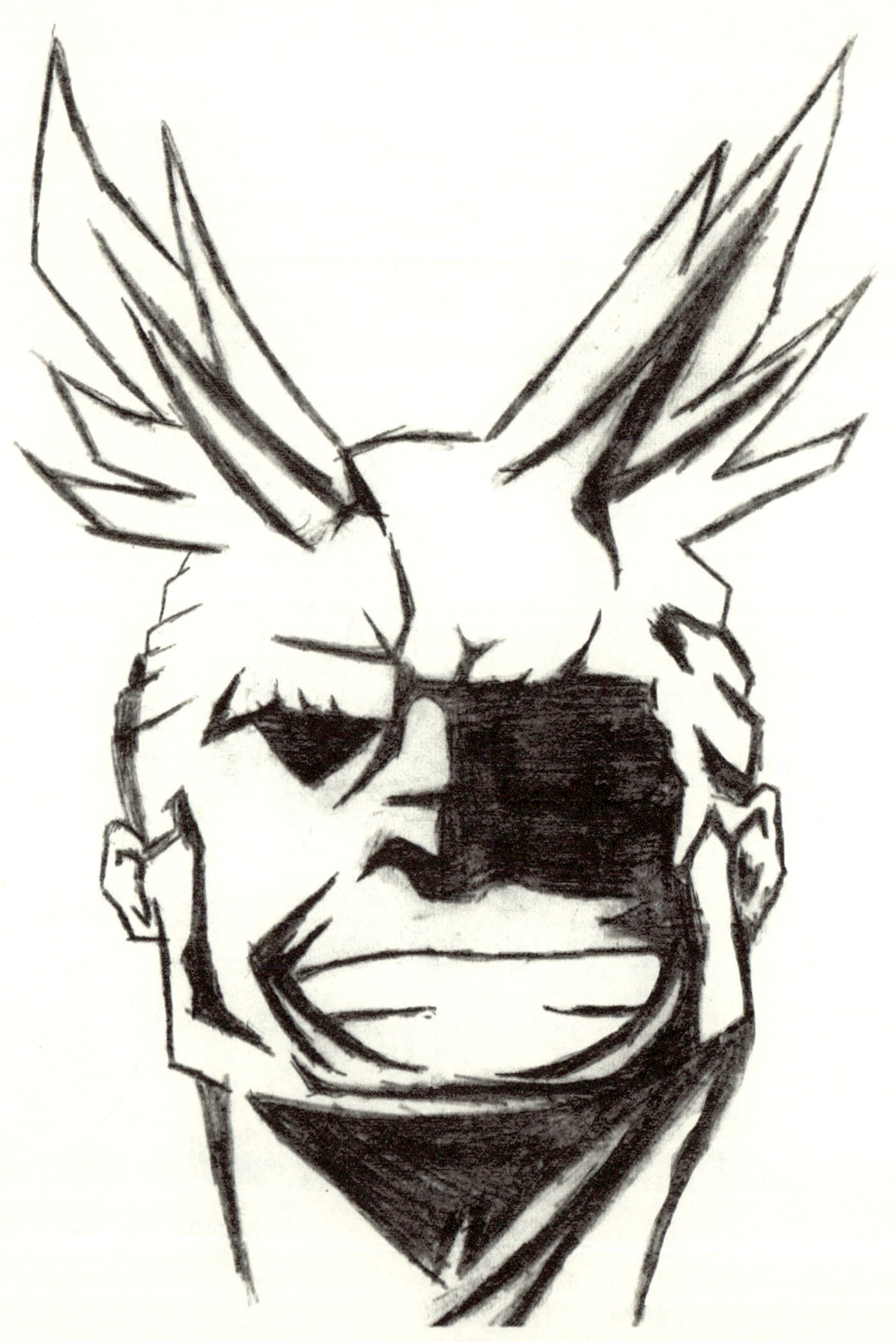

Tanaysha Chappell

5 The Fruit of Injustice

See Ya!

Shekynah Moore

I'll see ya when I can.
Maybe after this war or not.
It depends on what happens.
Maybe if the people stop chasing me,
Then I can see ya.

I'm sorry if I don't make it.
I was trying my hardest,
But with the guns around the corner,
I was too scared to leave.

I'm sorry if I don't see ya when I can.
It's not my fault the world doesn't
Accept me for who I am.
I don't care if we are in different colors.
I want everyone to love one another.
I'll see ya when I can.

We the Citizens of the US

Da'Onna Watson

We fight for what we believe and accomplish,
Our goals by any means necessary.
We demand our independence to this day.

The government has failed us with leadership,
So now it's up to us.
No matter the circumstances, we won't hesitate
To use force or fire.
Peace is a prophecy only commenced
To those who deserve it.

Our kindness and patience have been abused.
War is on the rise now.
Unagreeable and dishonorable leaders
Reflect amnesty and disrespect.
People die in cruel wars. For what?
A reflection of wrong thoughts?

Racial decisions? Oppression?
Unexcused deaths?
All for the Nations that aren't in our favor.
We still stick up for our country
Regardless of the mistreated citizens.
We are the people of the U.S,
And we will forever defend our country.

Daily Struggle

Andrea Ramirez

Their lives are being destroyed every day.
They are being separated from their families
With no hope of seeing them again.
Not today, not next year, not in ten years, possibly never.
Not knowing what's going on is the worst feeling.
We are like lions in a cage that are
Waiting for that one moment.

You can't have the hope of seeing them again
Because you don't know where you are,
Or what is happening to you.
They see us struggling without food and water.
While we are here suffering, they're enjoying it
As if we were a reality show.
But they don't care. Because we are just
Little animals sitting in a cage, defenseless.

They can't put themselves in our shoes,
But yet we are asked to put ourselves in theirs.
How are we supposed to respect them
When they are treating us like objects?
We can try and try all we want,
But we will end up in the exact same place.
They don't care about us. As long as they are
Safe and completely fine, we are
A piece of nothing to them.
Why try?

We Work the Same

Andrea Ramirez

There is no reason for us to
Get paid less, but we do.
We work the same, We put the same effort in.
We are capable of doing the same jobs as them.
Yet we never get the chance to.

Why? Because we are seen as less than them.
Because we are seen as "too weak."
Because "we can't handle it."
Because we are incapable."

But they are wrong.
We are capable of it.
We can handle it.
If they would open their eyes
For a second,
They would see that there is
No difference in our potential,
Yet we are sitting here,
STILL getting paid less,
Treated poorly,
For doing the exact same thing.

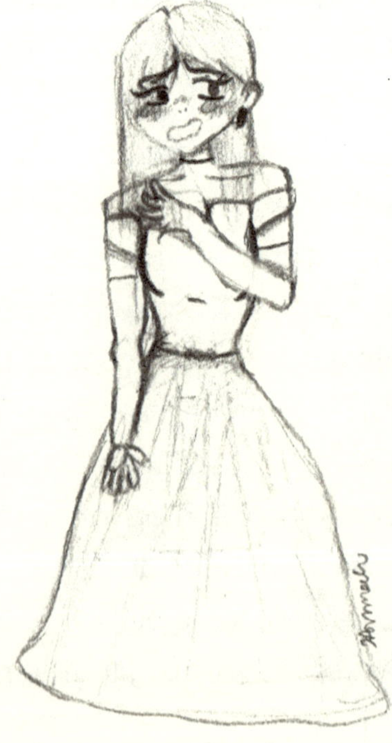

Hannah Jones

Cruelty

Karolina Blanco

It is cruel for the people who make up our population
To sacrifice everything they have, and then just get it
Thrown away as if it was nothing. Walking around
And being called an "Immigrant" in a place where
You thought you would be able to work hard
And find peace.

Can you give them a chance to tell their story?
Can you try to understand them?
Can you, instead of judging, help them?
Can you hear them out? No?

But why? Is it because they are immigrants?
Is it because they are defenseless?
Is it because they have no voice in the USA?
Is it because they aren't documented?

Not everyone should be judged by one person's actions.
One mistake becomes the blame of all immigrants.
Immigrants is just a word,
It is not a description of a person and who they are.

Leave us Be

Shekynah Moore

The children march
While their parents watch.
The children scream out feelings
While the parents give out beatings.

The children are dying,
Yet no one is trying
To make it right. The children see no light for the future.
The children look out for themselves,
While the government does the same

The children are killing themselves.
The government doesn't care they're playing their little game.
Their game of life where no one is right.
While the children see no light for their adventures.

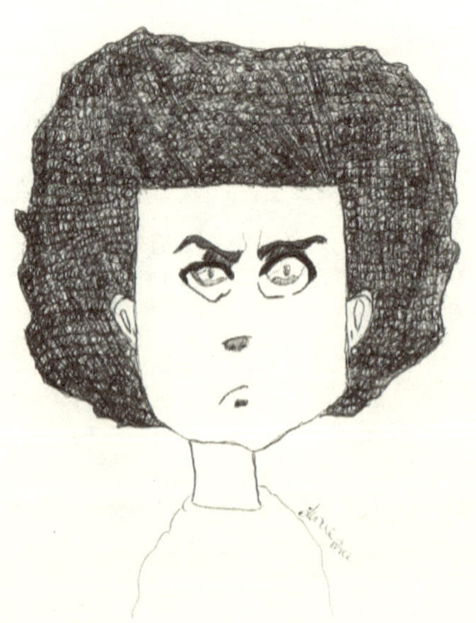

A Woman's Thinking

Alajah Thompson

These women are not getting treated
The way that they should be treated.
They get paid less
Because they are women.

Get talked to like they are children,
But they are not.
Get pushed around
Because of the way that they look.
It's just not right.

They get talked to like they are some dog and
That is not cool,
Because women try their best every day,
And they still get treated like they are nothing,

Like they can do things like men can do.
Like they are not capable of doing something a man can.
And this is something that is still happening to this day.
And it needs to stop.

Come To An End

Annabelle Lockridge

The world has come to an end again.
We see families dying from the inside,
Yet they still sent us back.
Families have broken apart because of paper.

Paper is the only thing that can keep us here.
You cry when you see the light.
You hide from the light.
You might even die.

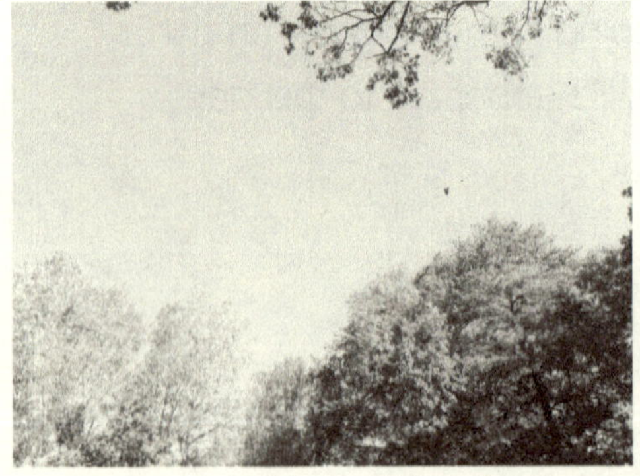

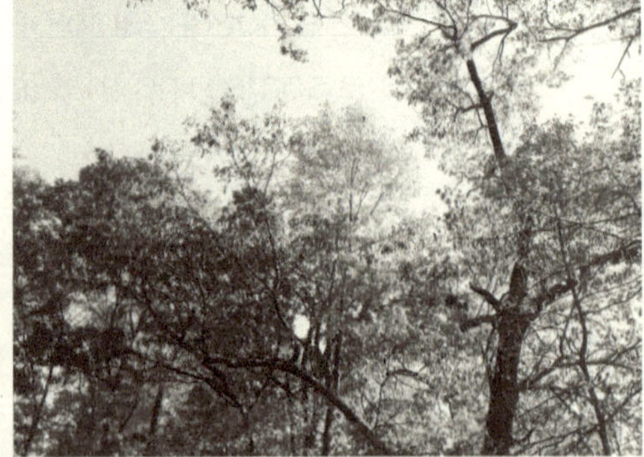

Brisly Esser

What's the Difference?

Jose Ortiz

Men and women are people
Just like boys and girls.
They both work,
And they both are living,

But why don't they get treated the same?
What if they were treated the same?
It would be equal for both men and women,
But not everyone thinks that they should be equal.

If they were to be treated the same,
This would settle some debates.
This would also give many changes.
They will all be doing new stuff
Because of the abilities they have.
Because they would all be equal.

This Is Love

Bradley Perez

Say it proud and oh so loud,
Love is all that matters now.
This crime and hatred,
It's all I've hated.

Understand that it's not strange,
And no I will not change,
For this is me,
So let me be.

Closeted or out,
I know that there's a crowd
That will yell out loud,
"We are proud!"

Understand that this is love,
Not just something that's made up.
For everything will change,
And I will stand so proud.

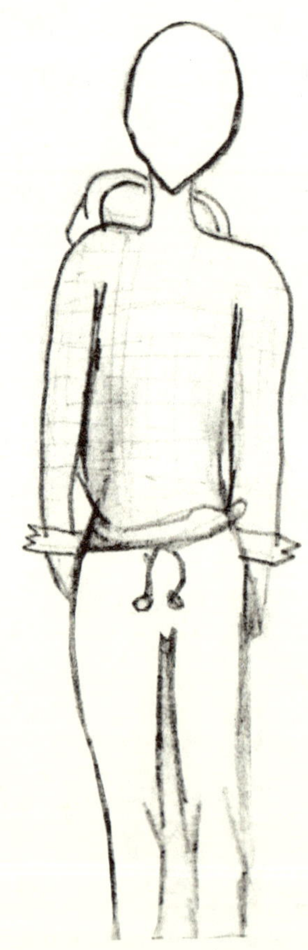

Tanaysha Chappell

Woman!

Alajah Thompson

A woman is powerful.
Women are strong.
Women are brave,
And will do anything.

They are gorgeous,
They are caring,
They are not afraid of anything.
And when I mean anything, I mean anything.

Women are classy.
Women are fair.
Women are the way that they are.
And that will stay that way forever and ever.

Women believe in things that others don't.
Women see what others don't see.
Women think what others think.
They do things that others will never think of doing.

Contradiction

Bradley Perez

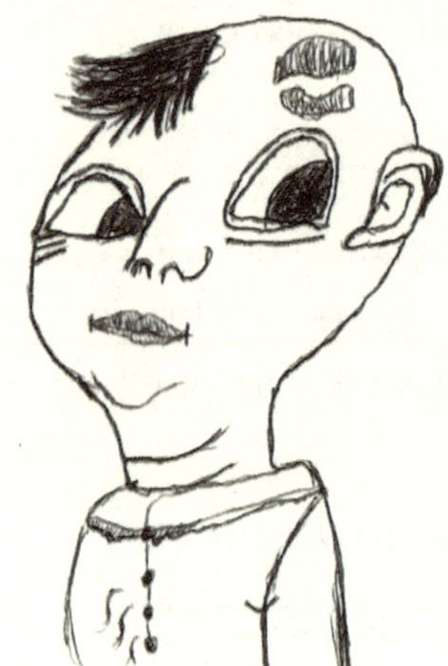

Homosexual, we say,
Straight, they yell.
The contradiction,
All the hate,
Wondering when it'll all just end.
Say we love.

Women are Women, Men are Men

Alajah Thompson

At the end of the day,
A woman is a woman.
And a man is a man.

We have different ideas.
Different mindsets.
Different thinkings of things.
We just need to come together,
As one, and stay together.
And stick with each other
For better or for worse.

Better for Them

Danna Texis

In search of a better life;
Not for themselves,
But for their children,
To give them what they never had growing up.

To provide them with a good education,
To have a roof over their heads,
Food on the table,
Clothes on their backs.

Growing up, they never had what their children did.
They sometimes came home with no food on the table,
Wore the same two shirts and shorts because
Their family could not afford anything else.

And dropped out of school at the age of eleven
To help out their mom with bills because
Their drunk father would never be home.
All they want is something better for their kids.

A life they wish they had growing up.
To never put their kids through
What they had gone through.
So they walked for months to be here,
And it's all of them, their kids.

The Battle to Stay

Danna Texis

We come here to stay.
But what? To stay in fear from those
Who want us out so bad?
The ones who constantly bash us for
Being illegals or undocumented?
The ones who always remind others
That we are the ones who ruined America?

We get shamed because of the
Supposed crime we have committed.
But this is no crime, this is surviving, this is fighting.
Fighting for everything we have,
And all the things we are determined to get in life.
We come here with no intentions of hurting anybody.

We come here to be better,
To get something we, unfortunately,
Could not receive where we were before.
If papers were not so hard to get,
Many of us would not be illegally crossing.

Abortion is Wrong

Annabelle Lockridge

The angry people crowded the hospital. They screamed and shouted about a subject they had never experienced.

"Abortion is wrong!" one man shouted

"Murderers!" another man screamed

They were mad at women for a decision they had made. They acted like the decision was easy to make. They acted like they knew what the women were going through.

They had no right to protest about this.

They had no right to make laws on our bodies.

I Fear!

Karolina Blanco

Maria walked for days thinking about my loved ones.

Her madre told her, "We are not always accepted but remember, you are going para un buen future."

Maria replied, "I fear I will never see you again."

She left behind her lifestyle for a new one. She mumbled to herself, "Will I cross? Are they going to reject me? Am I going to be accepted by the Americans? I don't know, but it is worth a try."

Love is Love

Bradley Perez

Every issue has a past that is still alive today.

Homophobia or general hate towards homosexuals is an issue that continues to this day. It forces people who just want to love to do horrible things.

I, being a homosexual, was always made fun of. I never really thought of it as being a bad thing. I never wanted to be made fun of and feel alone.

It is simply just a form of affection.

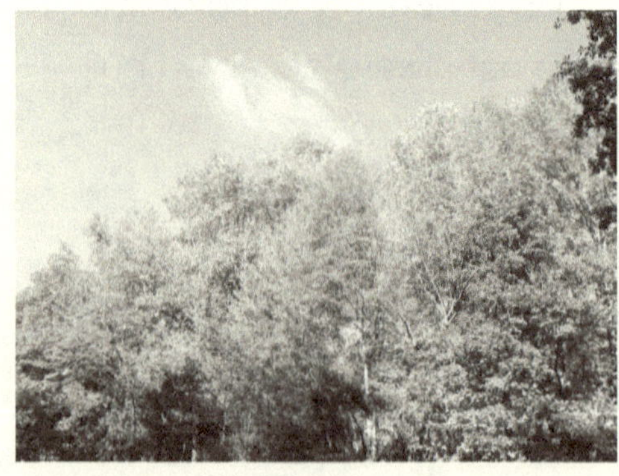

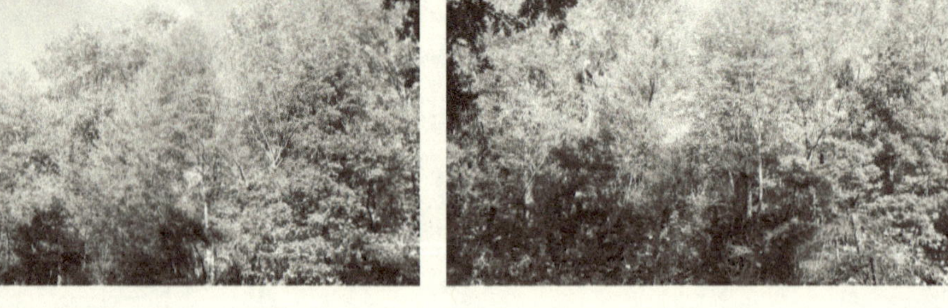

Brisly Esser

Not Prepared

Trevor Waring

Woe to ye who has not prepared.
Woe to ye who shall fail the grade.
Woe to ye who must drop out.
Woe to ye who has failed school.

Woe to ye who has no job.
Woe to ye who lives in a motel.
Woe to ye who doesn't socialize.
Woe to ye who is living sadly.

Woe to ye who has grown old.
Woe to ye who's family has forgotten about ye.
Woe to ye who spread no seed.
Woe to ye who's legacy is nothing.

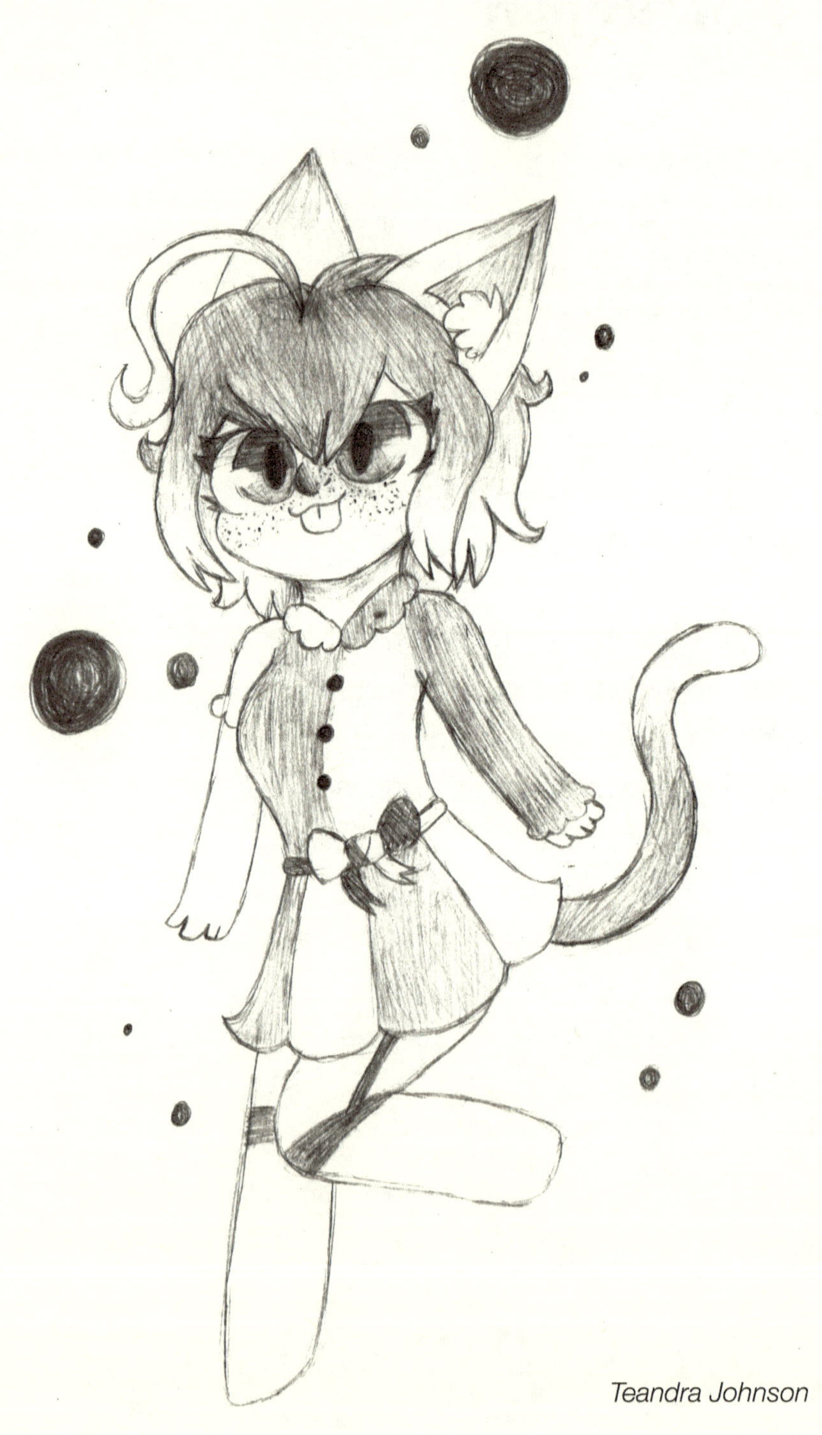

Teandra Johnson

6 Exclamation Points

Dress Code

Ja'berie Cobb

Why have a dress code in school?
Stupid clothes you have to wear.
Wearing the same colors all year long.
No expansion of colors to wear.

No one wants the same clothes as everyone else.
Can't wear hoody jackets,
Can't wear gym bags,
Can barely have any recess to play outside.

Never do anything fun.
Can't eat anything.
Feels like jail inside the school.
No one follows the dress code anyway.

Spirit

Victoria Doctor

Yes, my spirit is high.
Unlike yours, mine can never die.
I go too high and fly in the sky.
You stare upon me and say oh my.

But not everything lasts forever.
Even for the clever people.
But not everything lasts, no never.
All the people and whoever.

Yes, unfortunately, the mind can be broken,
And it can be caused by the one that's outspoken.
It can always be caused out of spite,
Even if your body was filled with such might.

Darkness may come upon you.
There are only a few that you may do.
Embrace it and never see the light,
Or smile to stand up and fight.

Today's Life

Muhammad Bouregba

All the same,
All the same,
Nothing new,
Nothing changes.

The lust to love,
Guns to swords,
Brick to metal,
Skin to the bone.

What more?

Life for death,
I think.
All the same,
Nothing changes.

More lives were taken.
More families lost.
More gunshots.
Never stops.

All the same,
Nothing new,
Nothing changes,
All the same.

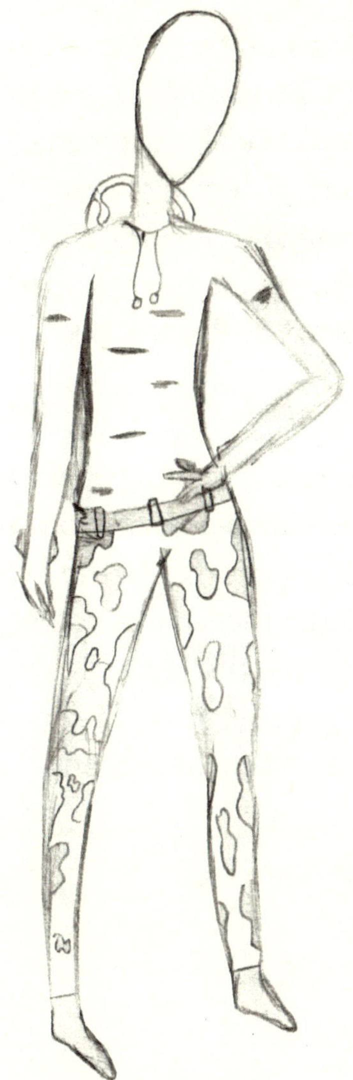

Tanaysha Chappell

Saint

Neida Hernandez

A saint so innocent but they always have a dark side,
Just wanting to feel numb to just get away for a little bit,
But because being a saint wasn't a role you took every day,
You were also the martyr.
Always putting others in front of you
Instead of yourself.
Feeling all the pressure falling onto your shoulders.
Didn't do you any good.

Feeling the way you felt wasn't at all good.
It damaged you, but did it matter? No, it didn't.
But did that bother you? Again, no it didn't.
So much time helping others you just couldn't save yourself.
So convinced that helping others would save you.
But you being the martyr and the saint you are,
You put your life on the line.
Soon it all went downhill.

From one day to another,
It was over.
The light at the end of the tunnel was just fading,
Your life being sucked right out.
What happened to all of the people that you tried to save?
Did they save you?
Did they give anything back?
Even a thank you?
You took the role of the martyr and saint but when you disappeared.

Where were all your saviors?

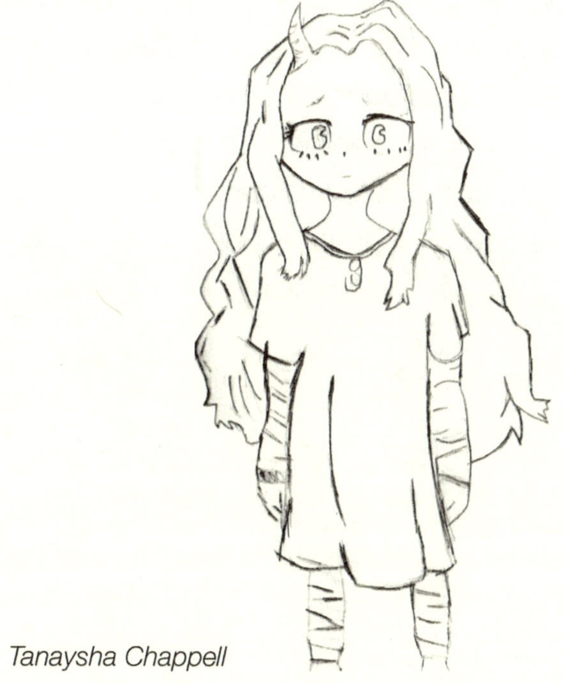

Tanaysha Chappell

The Anchor To My Ship

Monica Ramirez-Tanner

The anchor to my ship,
You held our ship down.
At the end of every day,
You brought us to treasure.
The anchor to the ship was strong.
Even if our anchor had to fight the tsunami
To hold us down.
You always took us to the port.

Our sea was strong and hard to fight,
Even if you had to push and push our anchor was
Strong, beautiful, and a fighter.
Our treasure was sweet and nice while it lasted.
Our anchor was strong, but so was the tsunami.
We loved our anchor but we knew
One day we would have to say goodbye.
We knew the day was coming soon.
We knew it would have been within a week
But we didn't know how soon it could have been.

Somehow we knew today was the day.
It was the day that everyone knew would come.
This battle of the anchor and the tsunami.
Everyone prayed and wish our anchor would win once again,
But we weren't sure this time.
The tsunami might have been bigger and stronger
But our anchor was still fighting to hold on.
The tsunami swings and hits our anchor right at the heart.
Our anchor let go.
Our anchor broke and our ship and treasure were lost.

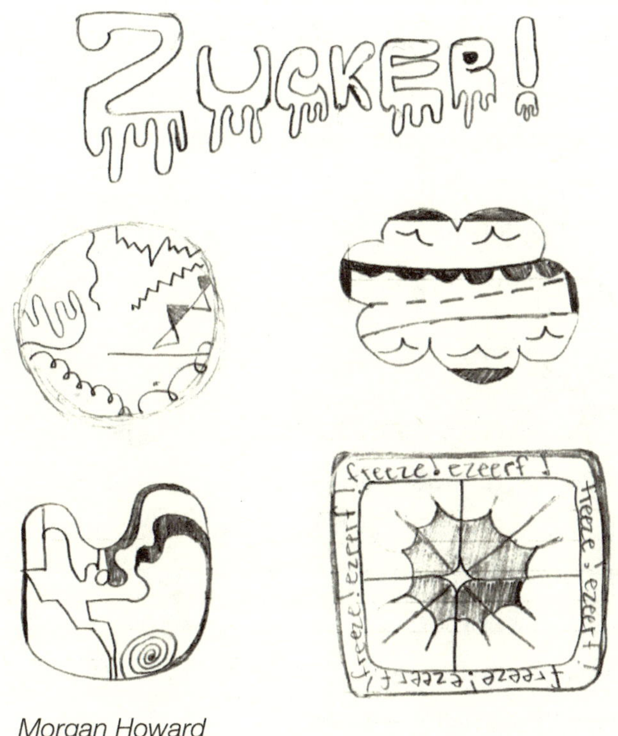

Morgan Howard

My Flower

Samantha Solis

My flower and her petal.
My flower would bloom, every time there will be new petals.
My flower will dance with the wind when sunshine hits her.
My flower will dance with the wind when the rain hits her.
My flower never looks on the negative side,
Only the positive.
So beautiful, so strong, so calm, and so caring.
I will forever love my flower.

My flower is the strength of her petals.
If my flower falls, her petals would fall with her.
If my flower felt happy, her petals would be happy.
My flower was really moody, but her petals never care.
My flower has fallen plenty of times.
My flower would put up a beautiful smile,
Nobody would forget her smile.
So beautiful, so strong, so calm, and so caring.
I will forever love my flower.

One stormy day,
It was raining so bad, that even the little bugs
Did not know what was going on.
My beautiful flower couldn't take it anymore.
My flower sank into the mud, her petals fell.
My beautiful flower died.
So beautiful, so strong, so calm, and so caring.
I would never forget my amazing flower.

I Admire You

Estefany Maldonado

Such a generous man filled with love and care,
For being a big and generous man,
For teaching me to be what I am.
For protecting and taking care of me.
For pushing me to keep going,
And teach us to follow a good example of life.

You went and left me a hole in my heart
I can not touch you but I feel that you are always with me.
I'm thinking that I'm not so far away.
Do not look for me so far that I'm close
Well, close to your side I'll hold you.

Every time you want to fall,
You can not kill a feeling
That you left me in my heart.
Your death was so hard and light
You went without but do not forget that I always love you.

I knew you as anyone,
Without realizing that little by little,
You went getting into my heart.
You are and you will be a special person in my life.
I always think about you but I do not show it,
And since you left,
You will always be the person that puts hope in my heart.
Thanks, man, for everything you taught me.

Convection

Anastazia Mendones

A convection current has spread across the world.
A temperature has progressed that isn't subjective
To idealistic terms such as hot and cold.
A mood has been established,
Uplifting the lives of the organisms on Earth.
A realization has been drawn
From the bounds of nothingness.

An escape from the hibernation and
Minuscule days that corresponds is accepted.
An epiphany that brings upon bright life in a dull location.
An overrated and misused chance for revitalization.
A complex event that is subdued and tied
To a word made to cover accusations.

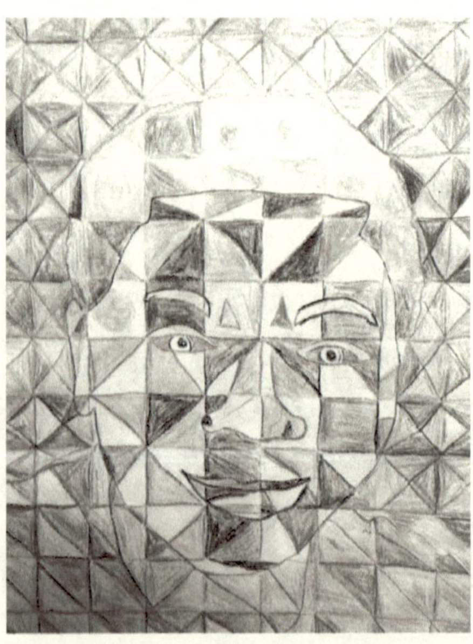

The appearance of plants that were dead
And hiding in the abyss underground,
The spread of warm air that caused a wave
Of eradication amongst its retreat.
The notification of the end of the world,
A promise that is tied to a timestamp,
The presence of a period humans
Have no dictatorship over.

Spring is regarded as one of the four-time
Dissections that comprise a year.
A phenomenon that occurs over
An indefinite three month period.
An example of recreation without
The involvement of humanity.
The basis of a schedule that has been engraved
Within Earth's core.

The Blandness Break

Victoria Doctor

Confined to this blandness once again,
All this lack of color makes my head spin.
Grey, black, and white is lame.
I say the school district is to blame.

We slowly rebel day by day.
They can't tell from their dismay.
We wear scarves and bandannas,
But hey, we aren't in Havana.

One day we will show them who rules.
Sometimes adults can be such tools.
We will rule the world one day soon,
But now it is time to play.

All of us will have lots of fun.
Soon one day the battle will be won.
We will all be soon full of cheer.
Everything is always near.

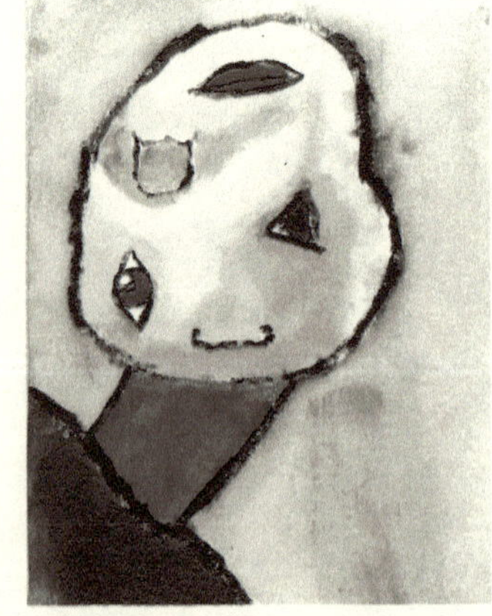

My Blue Jean Jacket

Priceless Johnson

My Blue Jean Jacket.
What did it ever do to you?
The buttons are all in the right places
Just like all of our beautiful faces.

My Blue Jean Jacket.
It's not as menacing as they deem.
There is nothing to worry about for its
An outer layer of confidence.

The beauty that lies within its threads
Does its job to keep me warm
From not just the cold but the haters
Because when I put it on, I am the GOAT.

So you see, My Blue Jean Jacket
Protects me,
Not from the element of weather,
But from the element of distress.

Sister Pollen

Meagan Brown

I didn't like Spring last year.
I surely will dislike it this year as well
Bringing horror and cringe down to my bones.
Spring whispers in your ear, secretly
Covering you with powder.

It's not the powder that some people like to inhale,
Its powder is the color of bright sunflowers
That everyone seems to admire.
Flooding the sidewalks and roaming the air,
Giving you a sneak attack resulting in a sneeze.

Having the disease-carrying children
Pass their sickness onto you,
Continuing the cycle forever while the doctor
Pressures your parents to vaccinate you,
I continue wheezing while my lungs are gasping for air,
The stalker constantly follows me trying to get extra love.

Liking the sight of the waterfall coming from my nose,
And the rose color of my eyes.
I wish for something else to love me instead.
It wouldn't be bad if a handsome bee
Came to give me
A small peck
On the cheek?

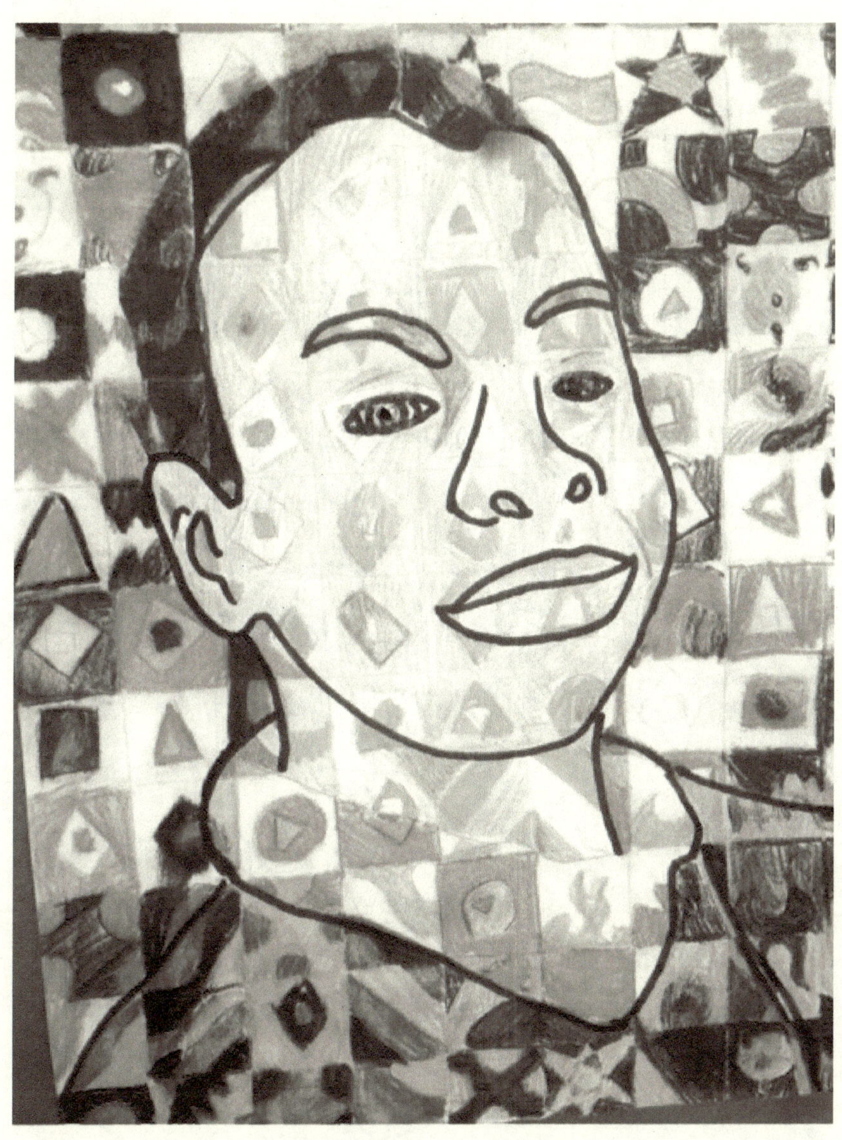

SANAZ IN TEHRAN

By: Edmirellys Merle Diaz

Edmirellys Merele Diaz

7 Oppression Session

Each year, the Honors English 1 class explores graphic novels and oppression by reading an excerpt from “Reading Lolita in Tehran” by Azar Nafisi and part of “Persepolis” by Marjane Satrapi. Then they take that excerpt and develop a “graphic novella” of sorts, using film techniques, perspective, and the like. In this excerpt, a young woman, Sanaz, prepares to cover up and walk home, unseen, in Tehran after reading forbidden literature.

We are pleased to present a few of our best examples of their hard work.

Enjoy.

Transformation

Bradley Perez

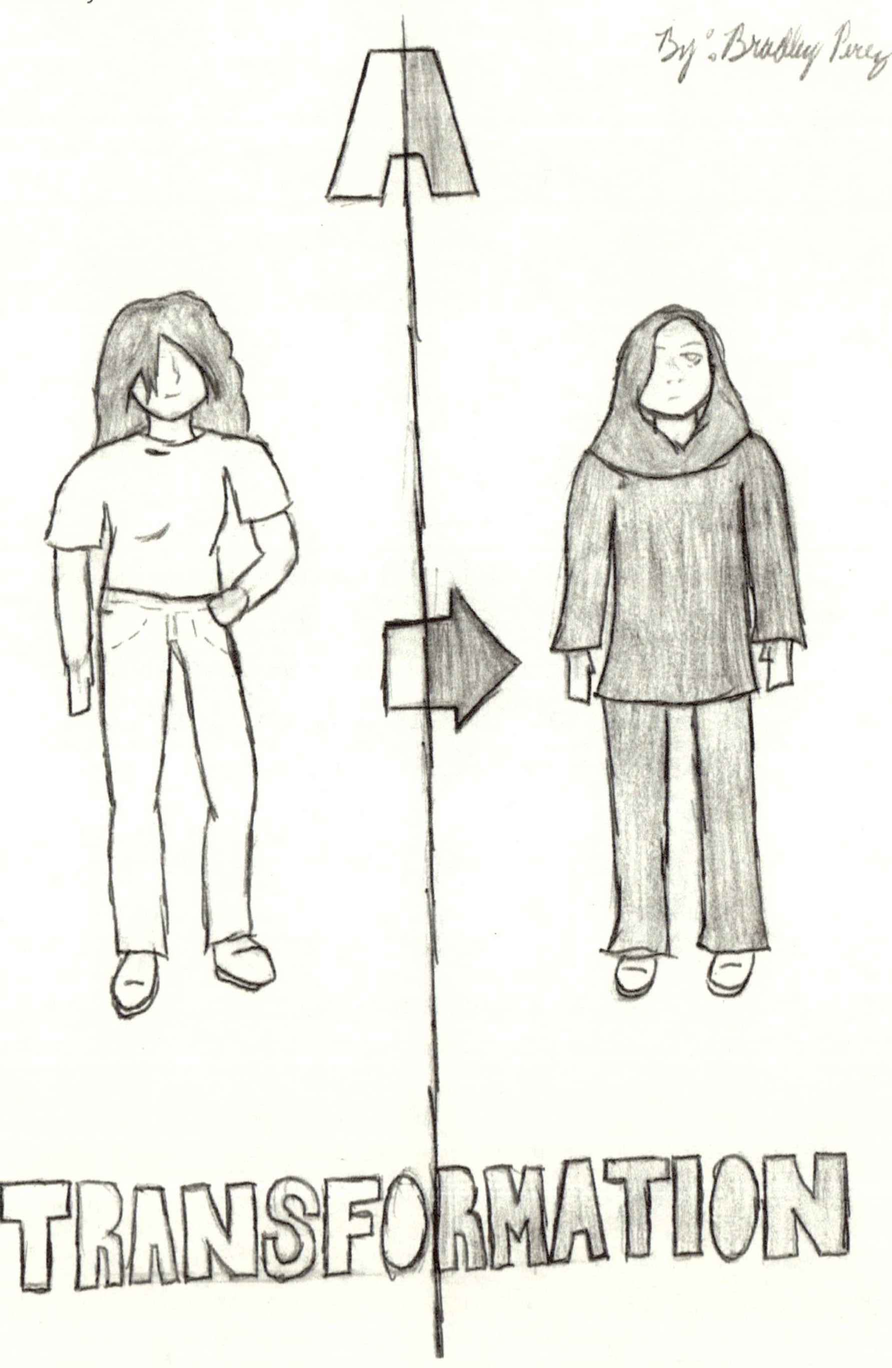

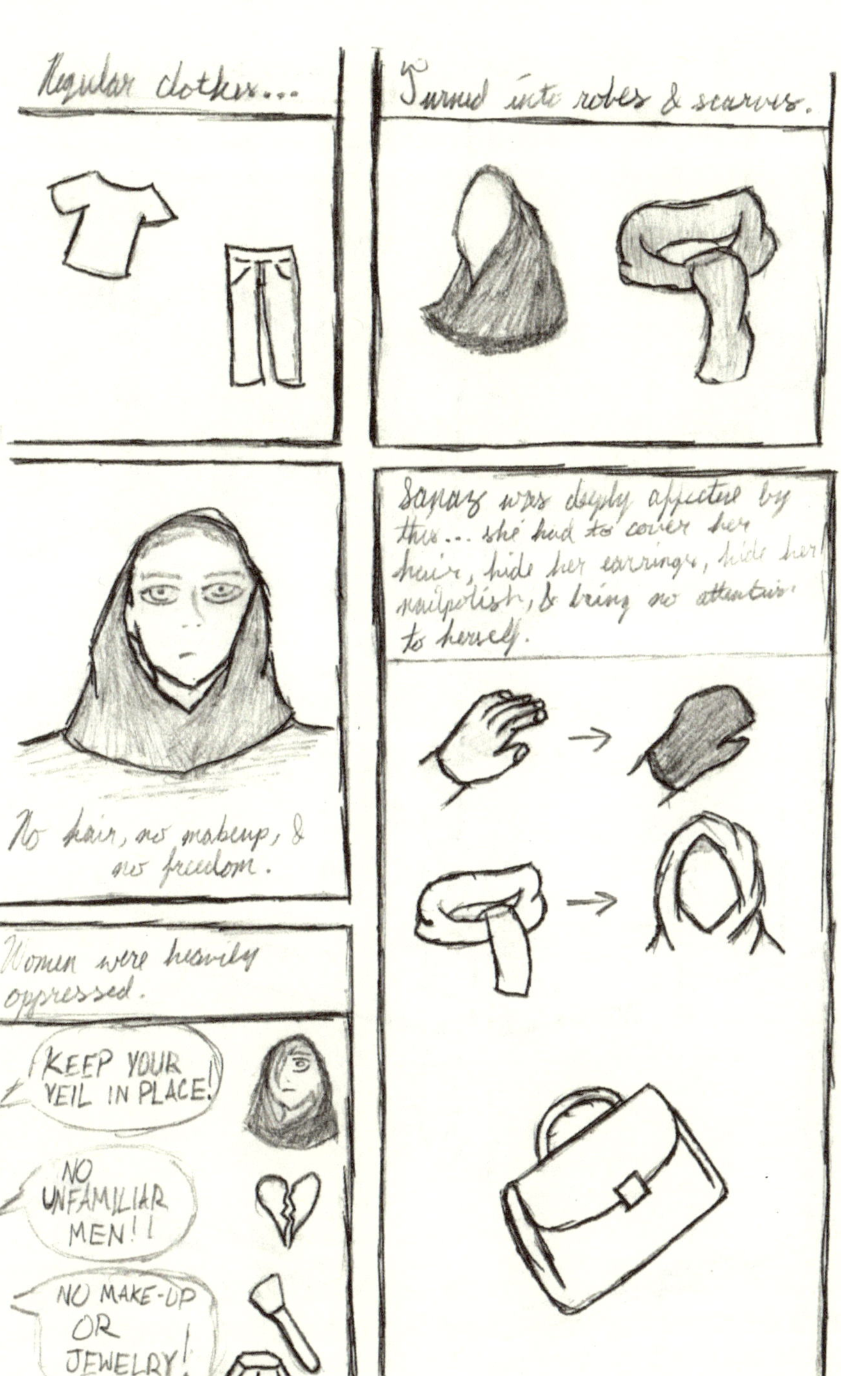
Regular clothes...
Turned into robes & scarves.
No hair, no makeup, & no freedom.
Sanaz was deeply affected by this... she had to cover her hair, hide her earrings, hide her nailpolish, & bring no attention to herself.
Women were heavily oppressed.
KEEP YOUR VEIL IN PLACE!
NO UNFAMILIAR MEN!!
NO MAKE-UP OR JEWELRY!

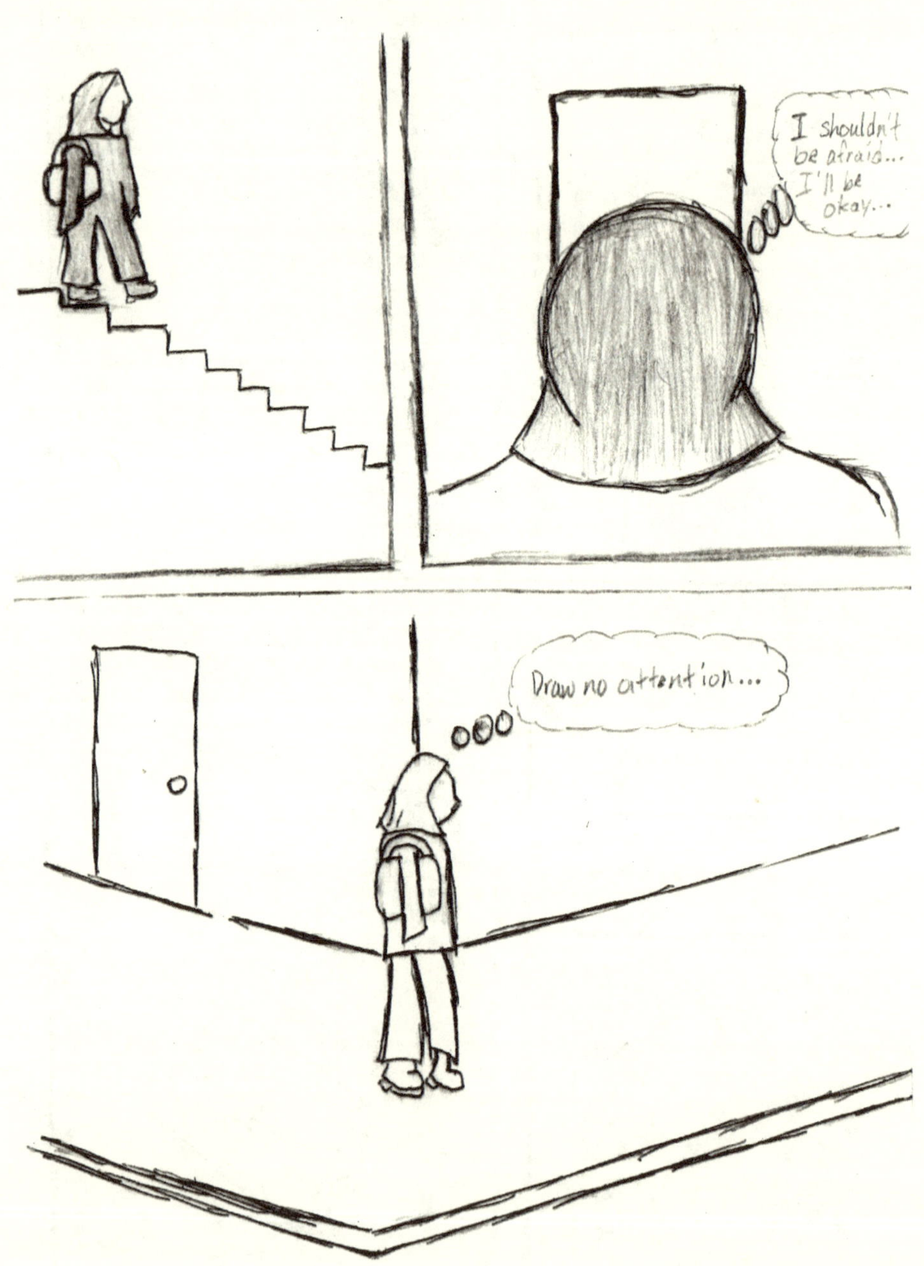
I shouldn't be afraid... I'll be okay...
Draw no attention...

MEN WHO WEAR TIES ARE U.S. LACKEYS.

VEILING IS A WOMAN'S PROTECTION

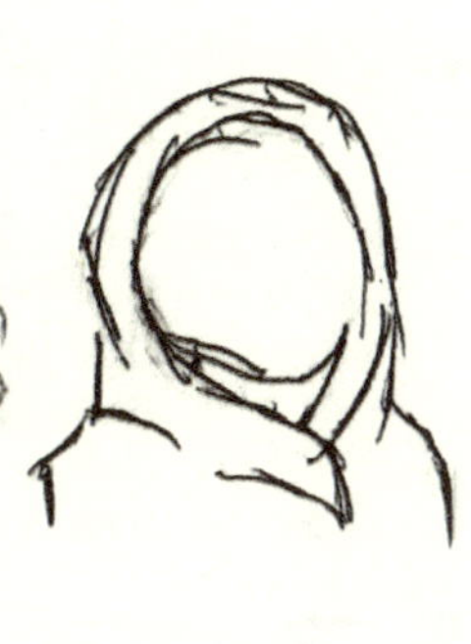

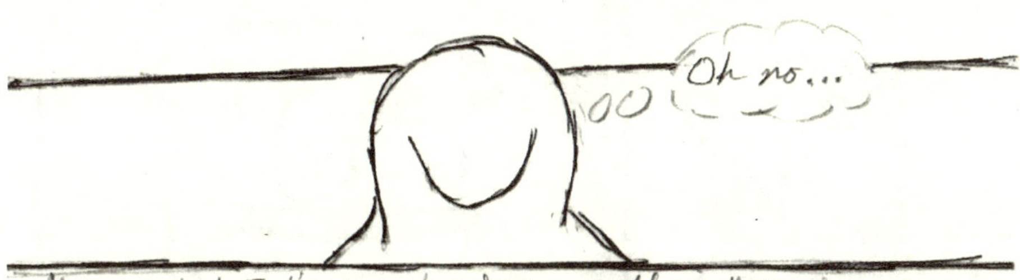

It was about 5 times a day Sanaz would see these slogans.

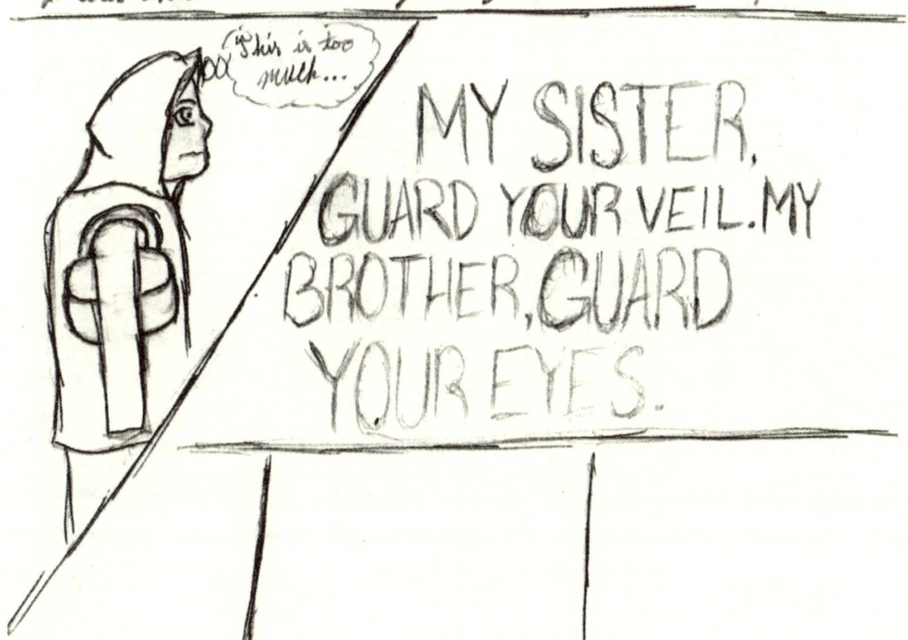

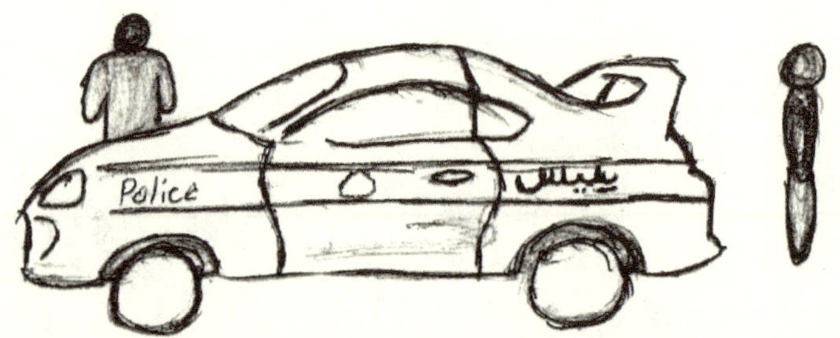

Everywhere you looked there would be some type of government power.

They'd look stern & forceful...

Made sure people knew who they were...

They would have weapons...

And force society to follow the rules.

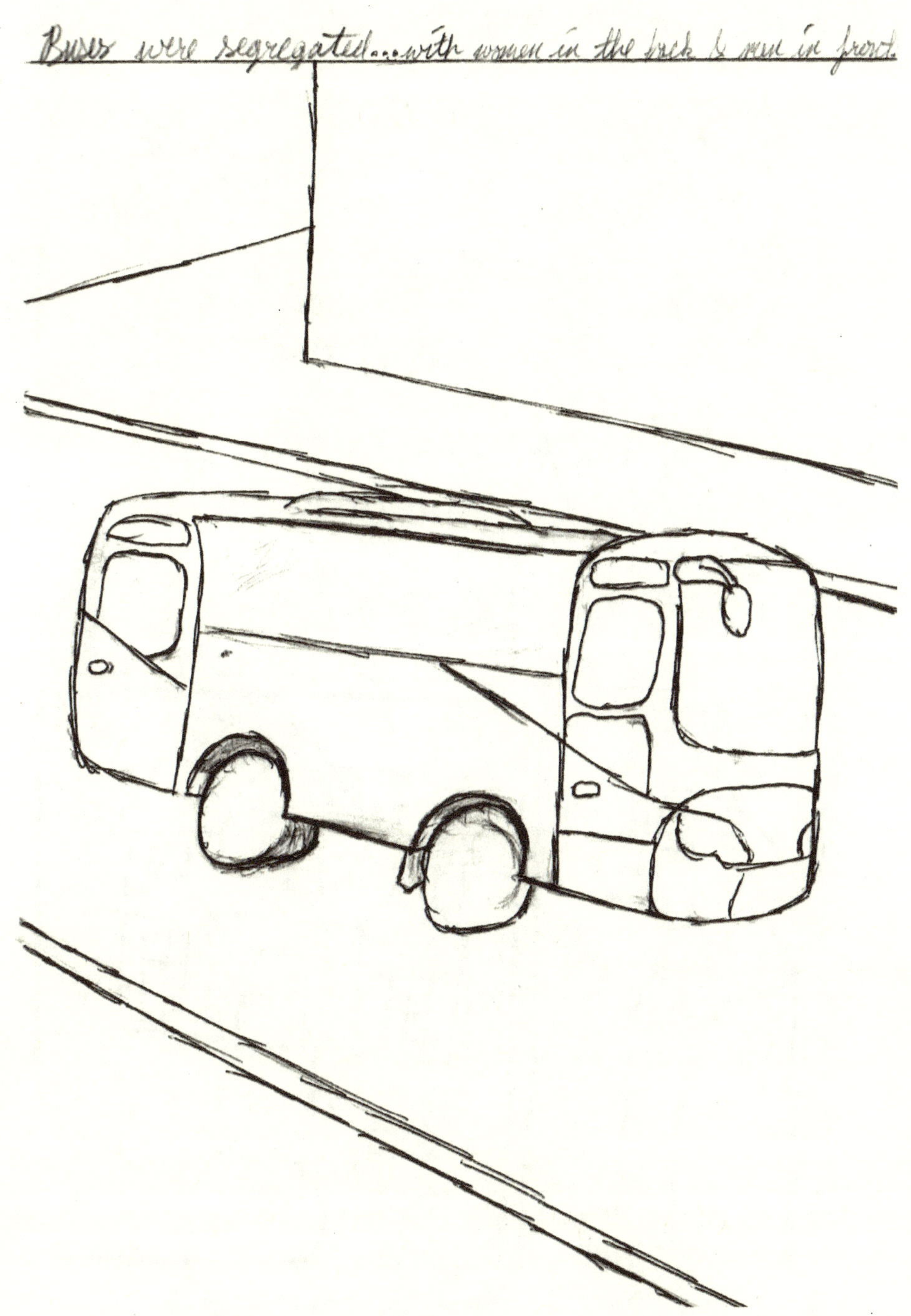
Buses were segregated...with women in the back & men in front.

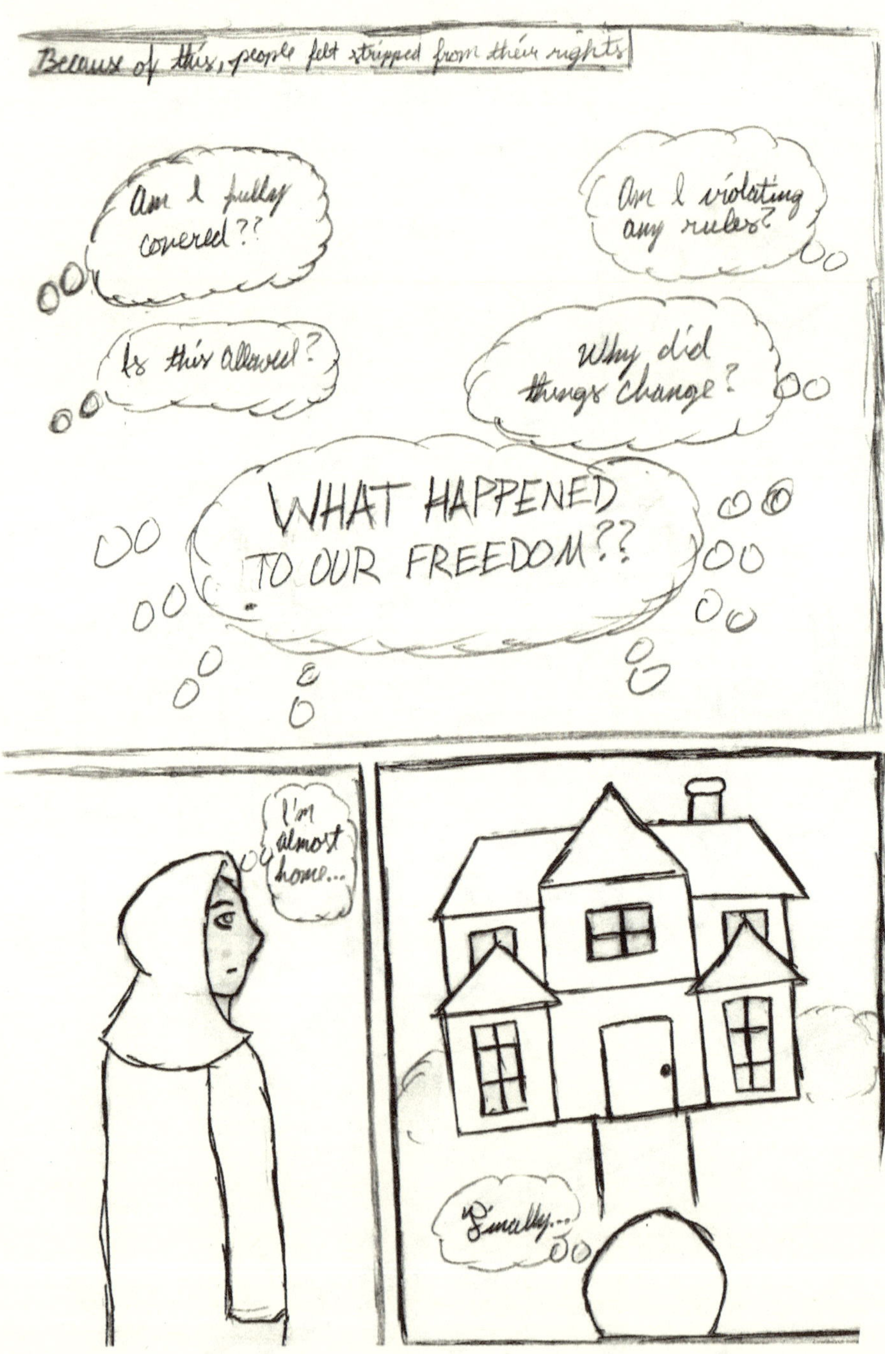
Because of this, people felt stripped from their rights
Am I fully covered??
Am I violating any rules?
Is this allowed?
Why did things change?
WHAT HAPPENED TO OUR FREEDOM??
I'm almost home...
Finally...

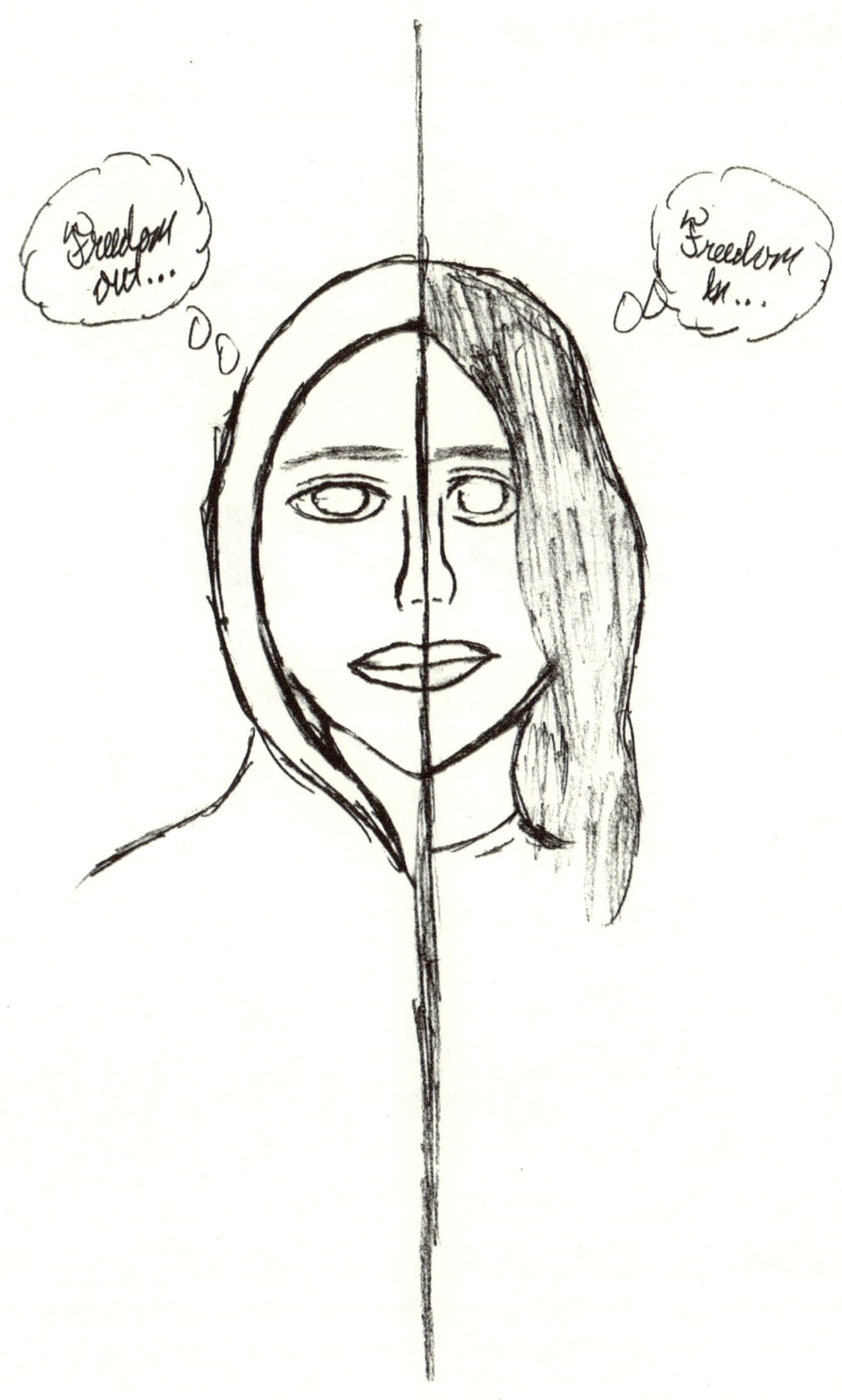
Freedom out...
Freedom in...

Underground

Jose Ortiz Avalos

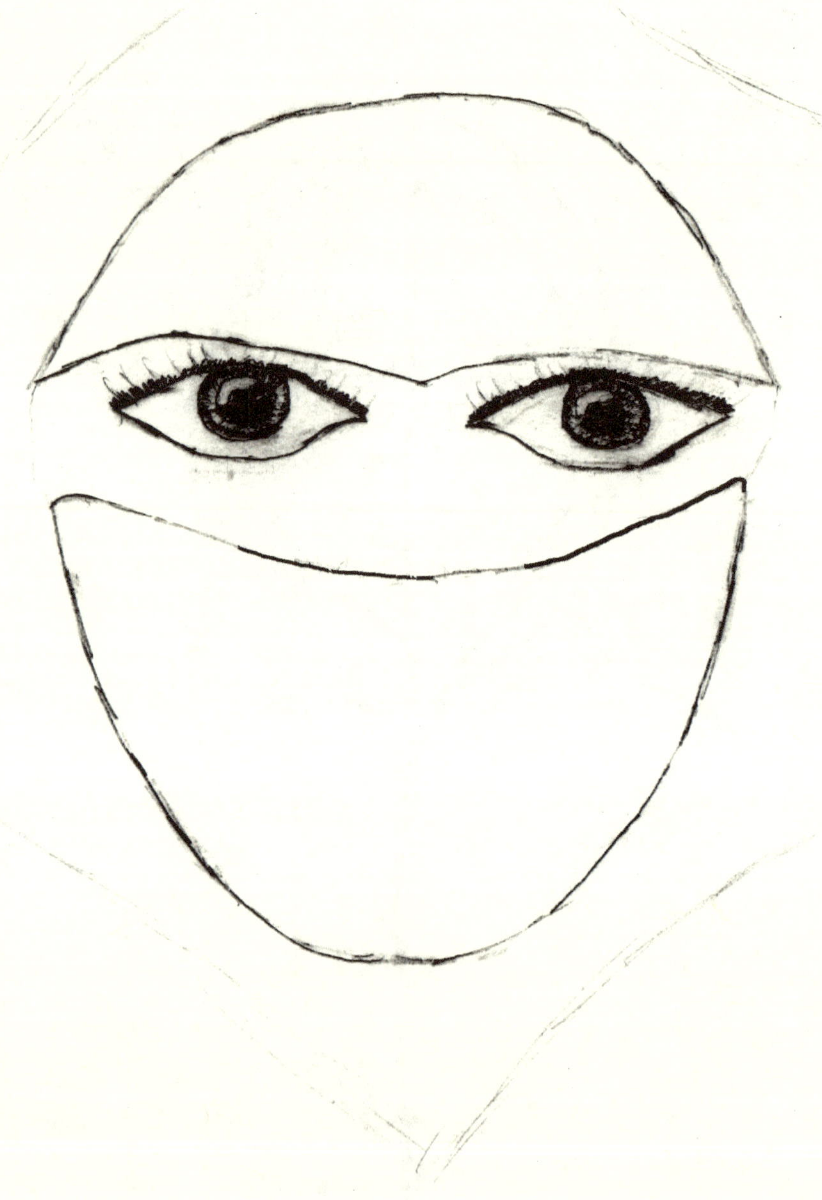

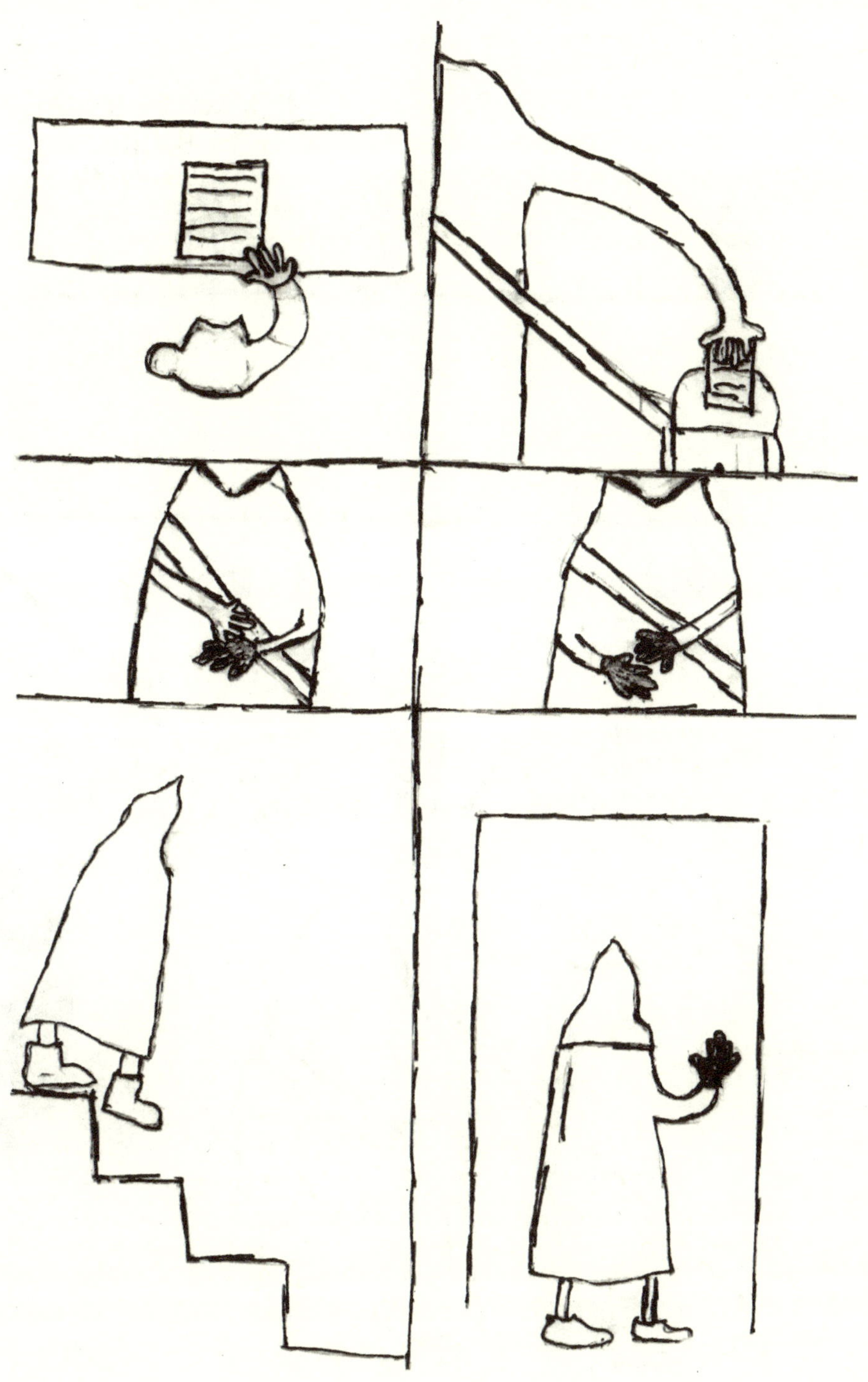

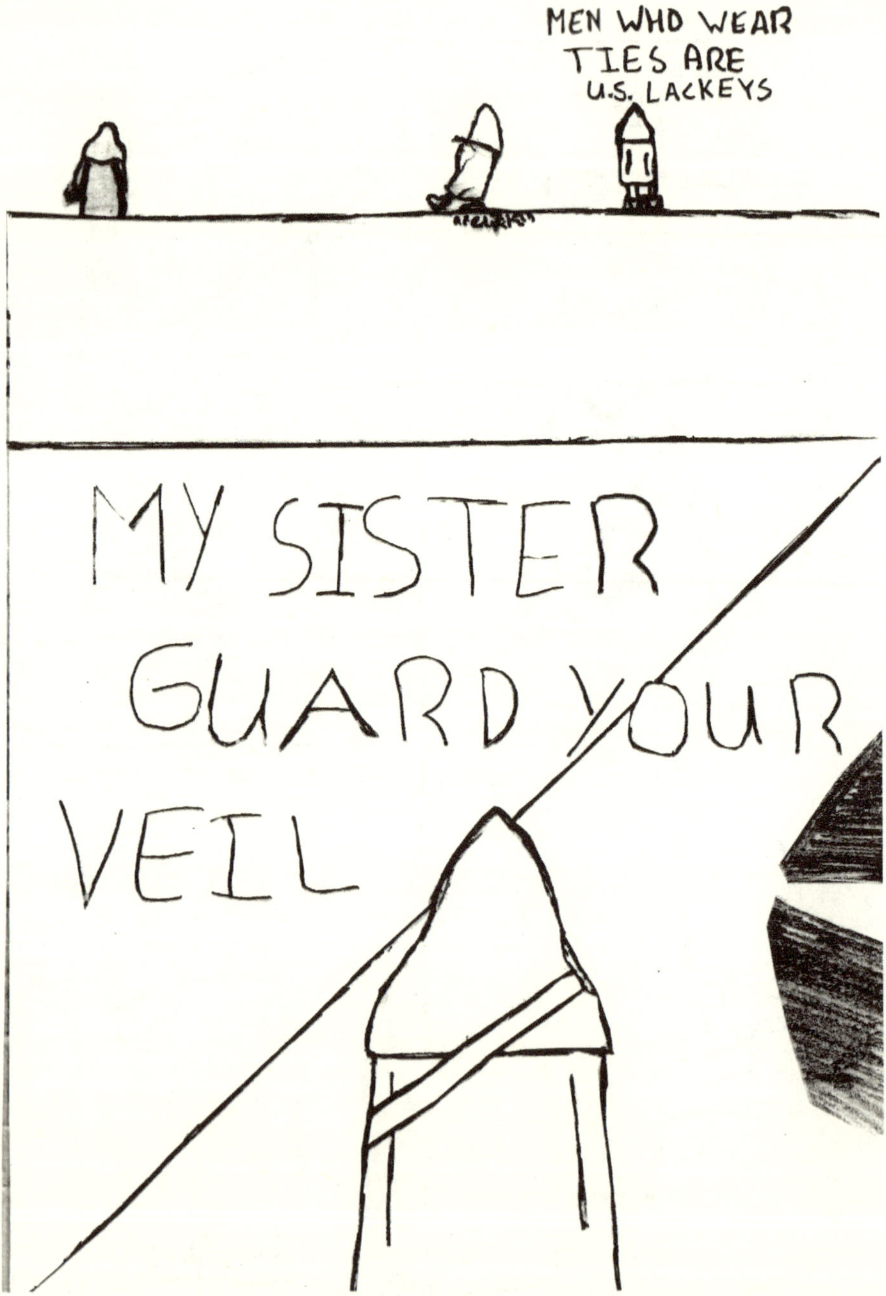

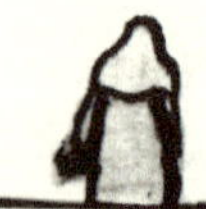

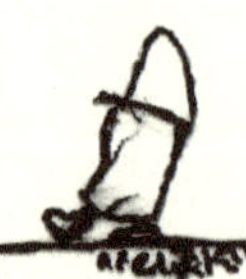

MEN WHO WEAR TIES ARE U.S. LACKEYS

MY SISTER GUARD YOUR VEIL

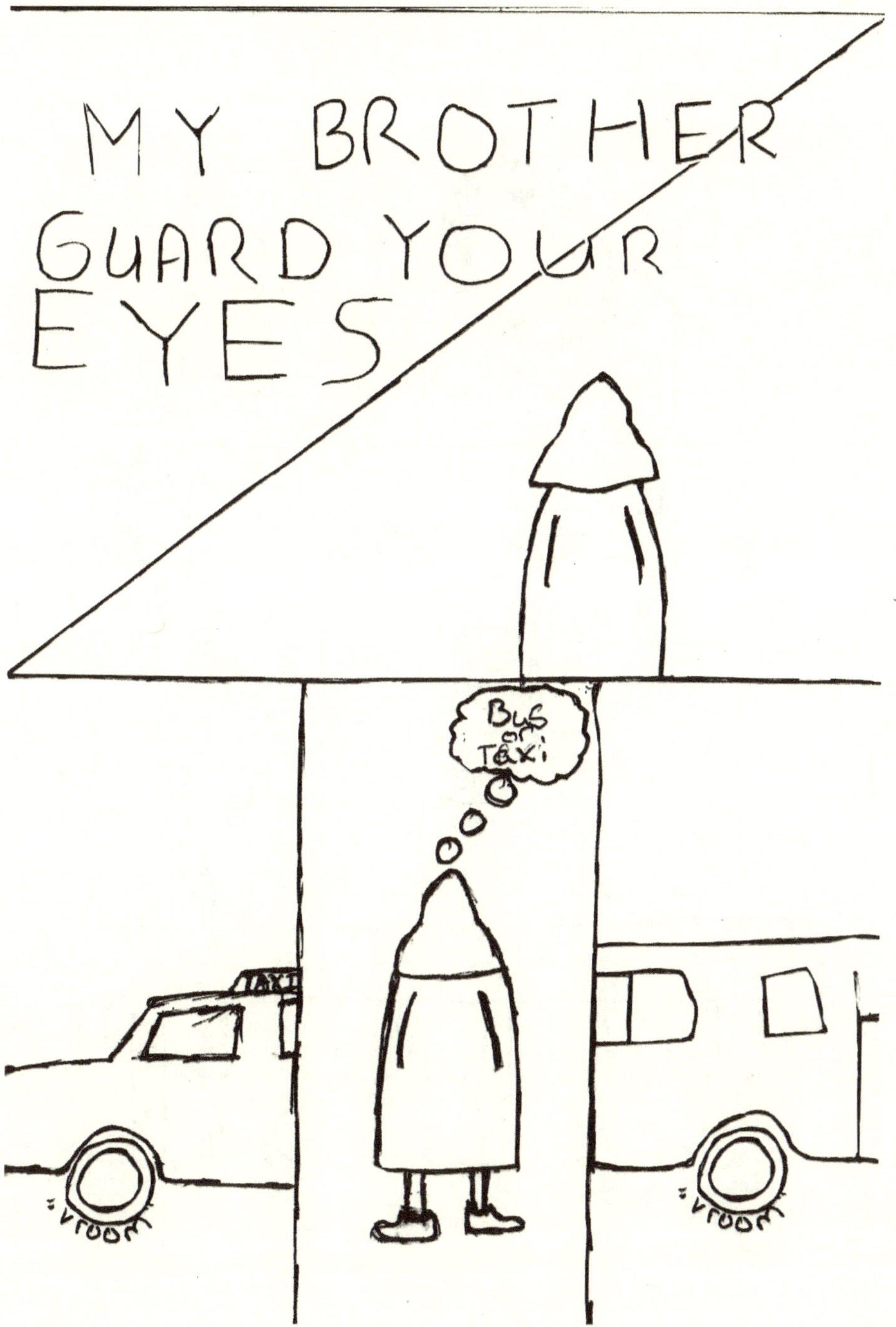
MY BROTHER
GUARD YOUR
EYES
Bus
or
Taxi
TAXI
vroom
vroom

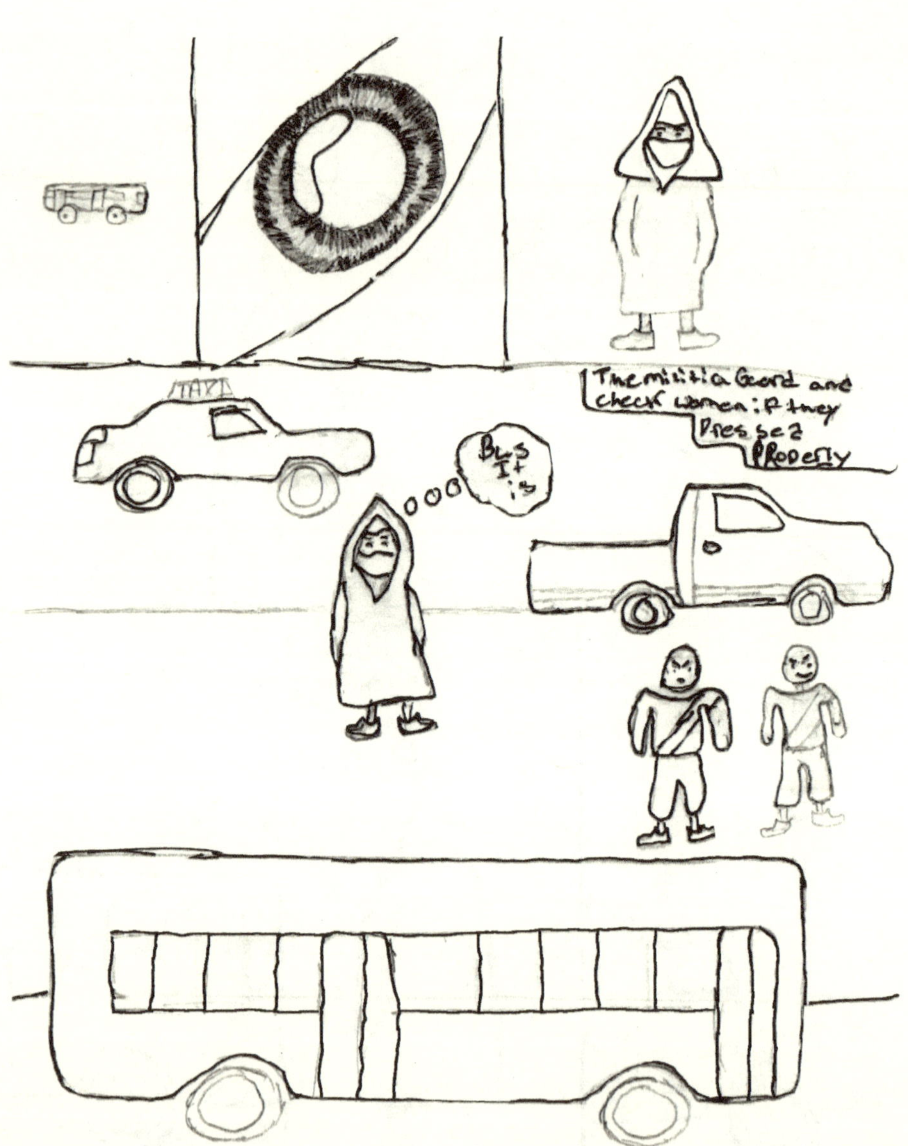
TAXI
The militia Geard are
checK women if they
Dressed
Properly
Bus
It
is

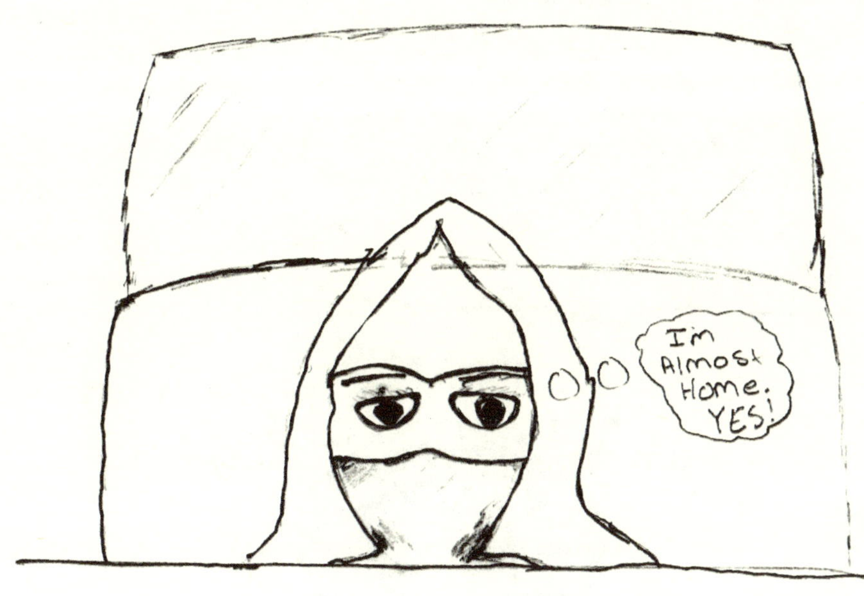
I'm Almost Home. YES!

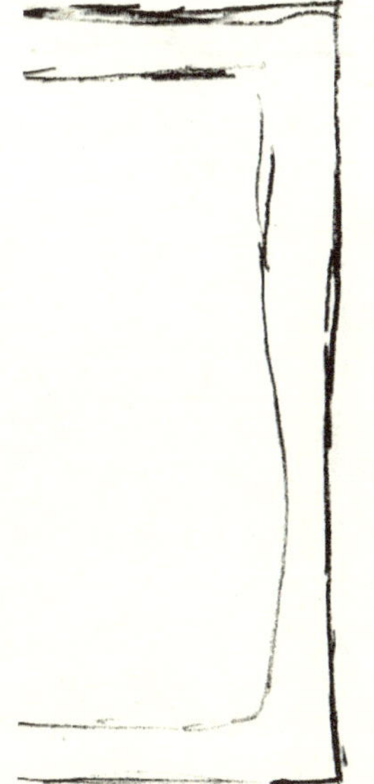

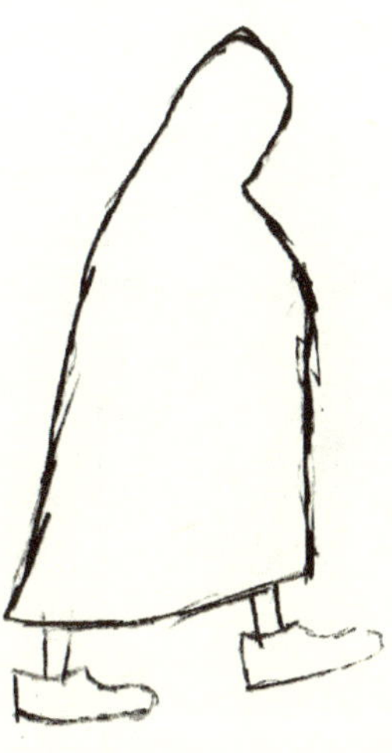

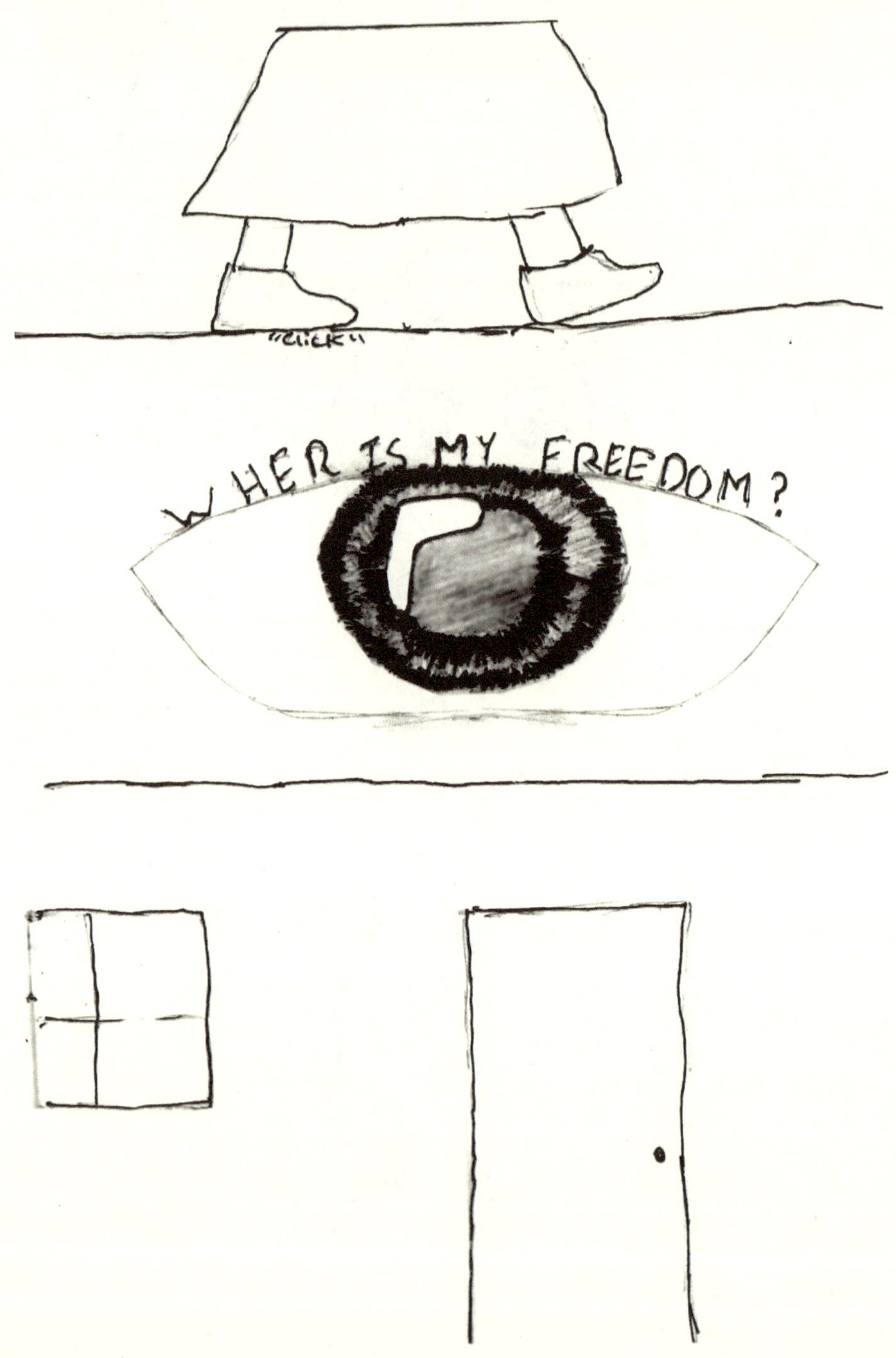
"click"
WHER IS MY FREEDOM?

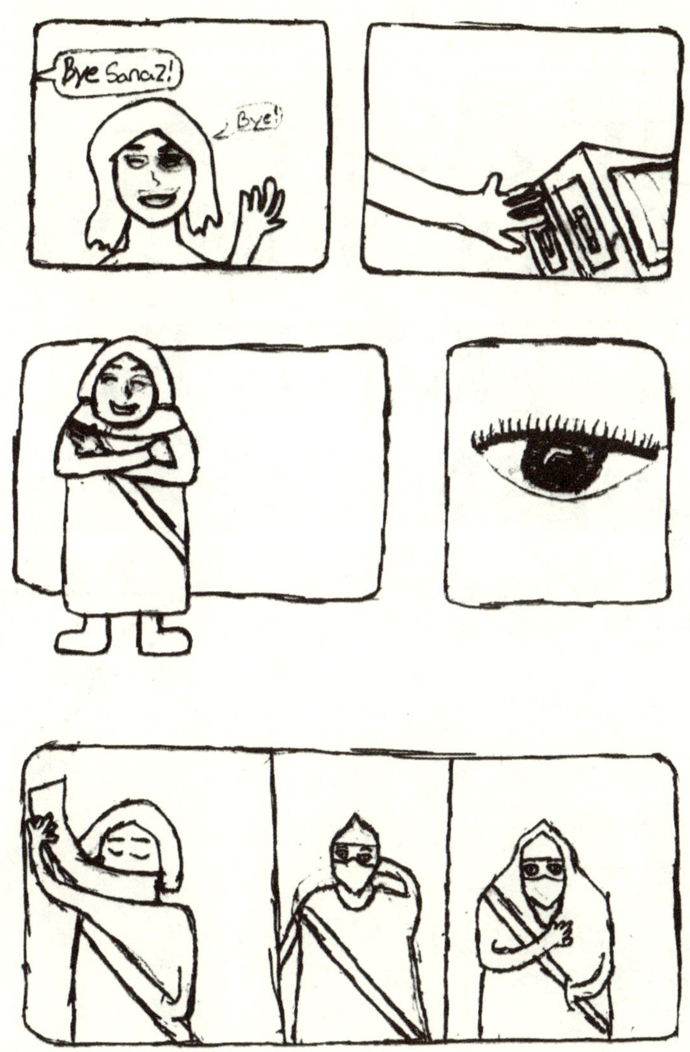
Bye Sanaz!
Bye!

Freedom

Karoline Blanco

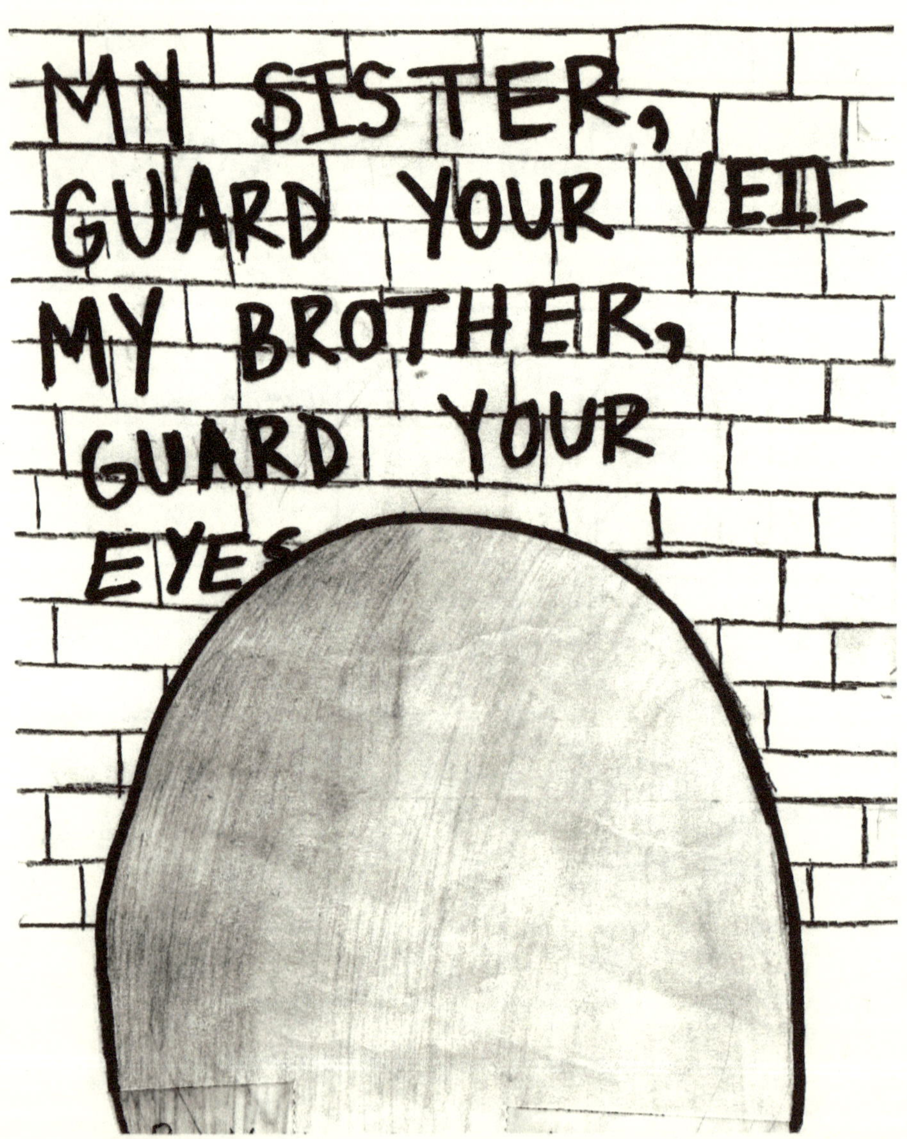

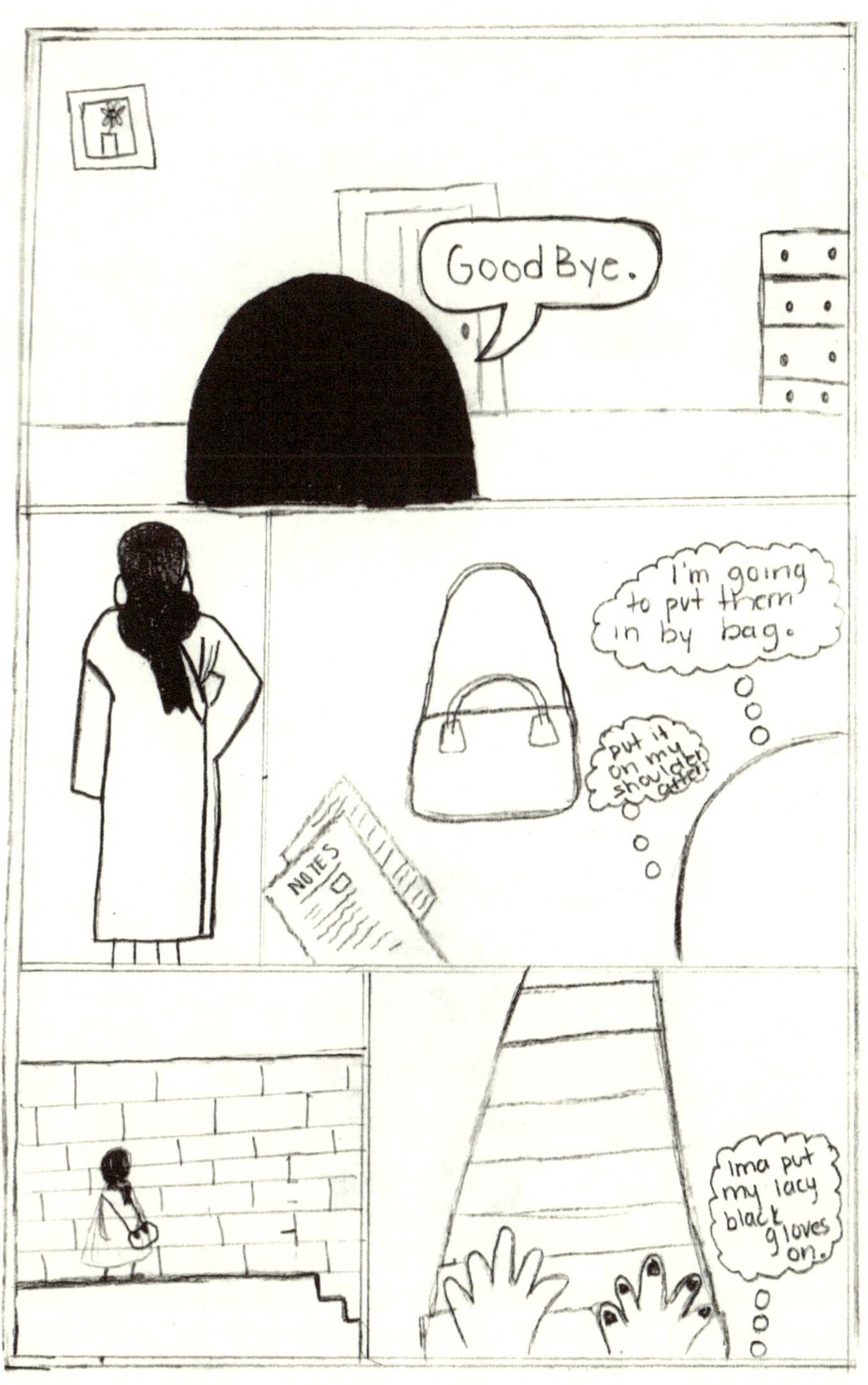

Good Bye.
I'm going to put them in by bag.
put it on my shoulder after
NOTES
Ima put my lacy black gloves on.

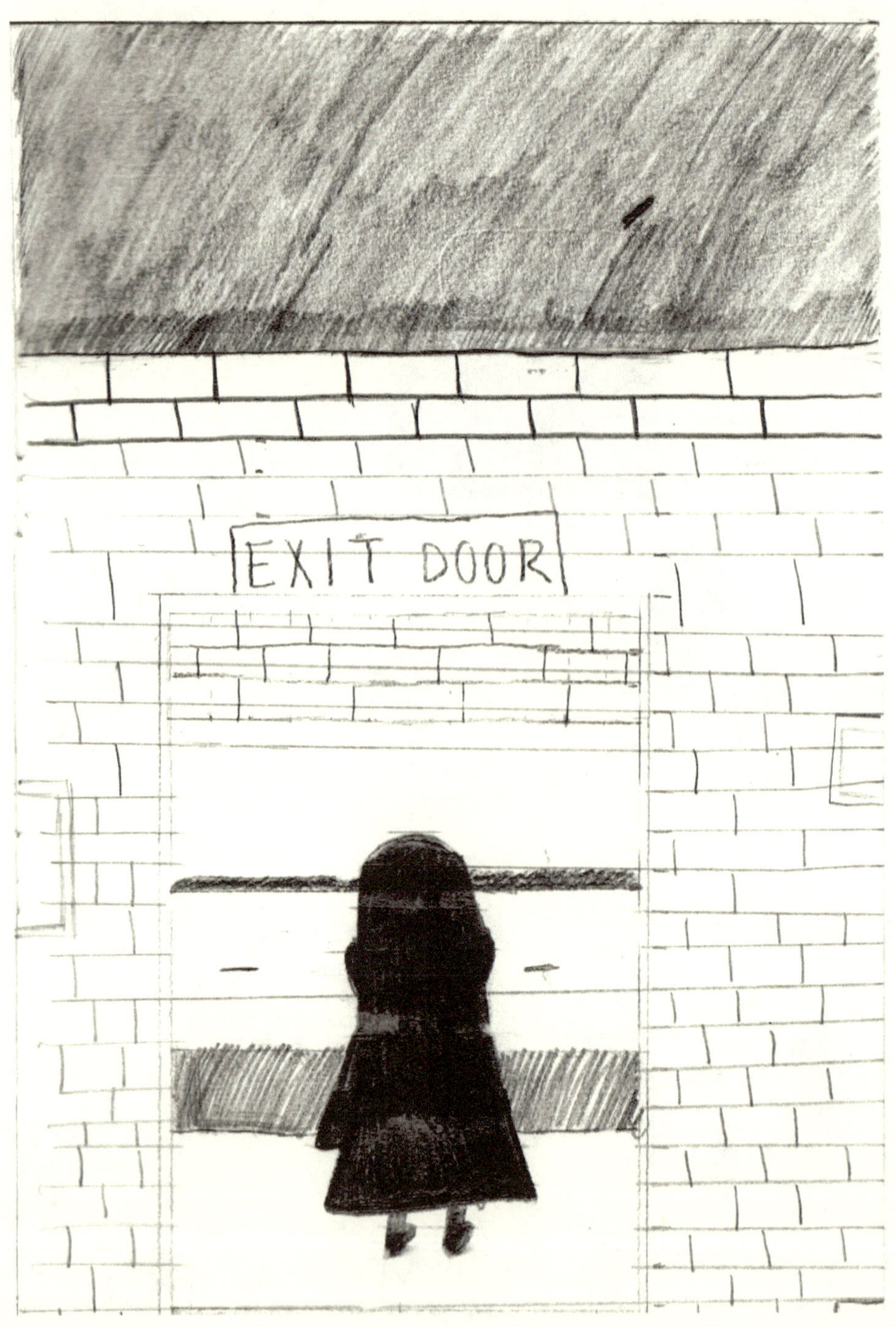
EXIT DOOR

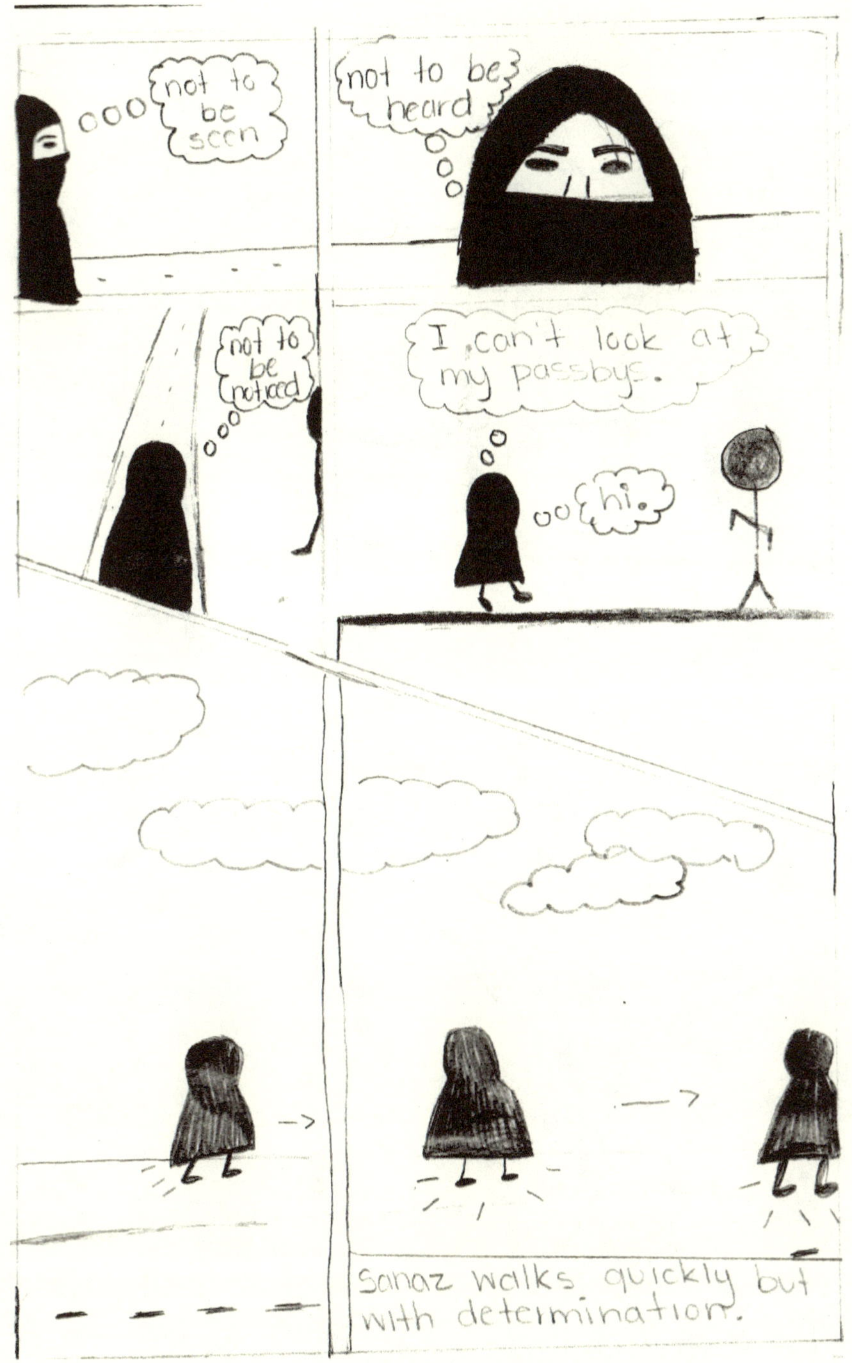
not to be seen
not to be heard
not to be noticed
I can't look at my passbys.
hi.
Sanaz walks quickly but with determination.

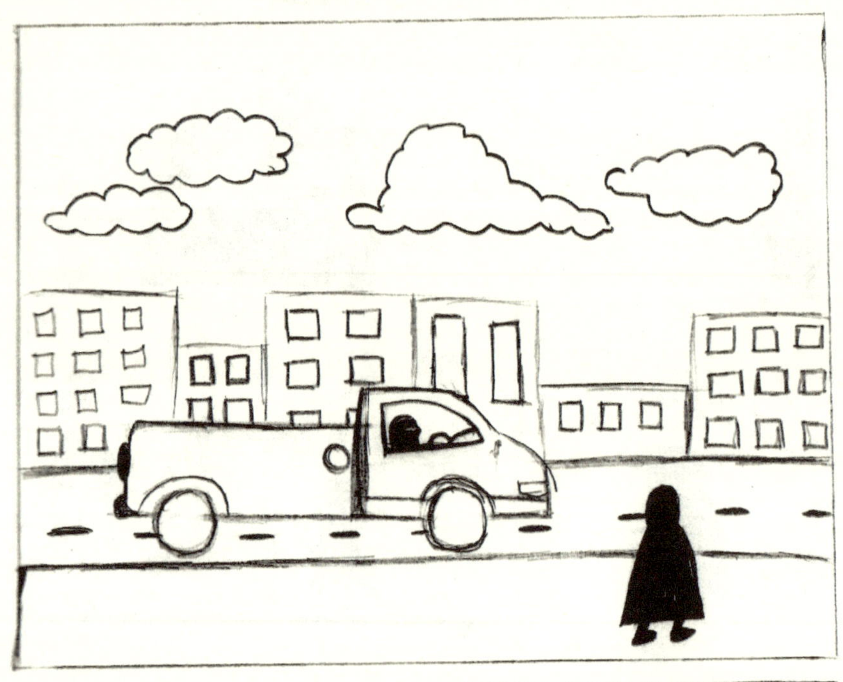

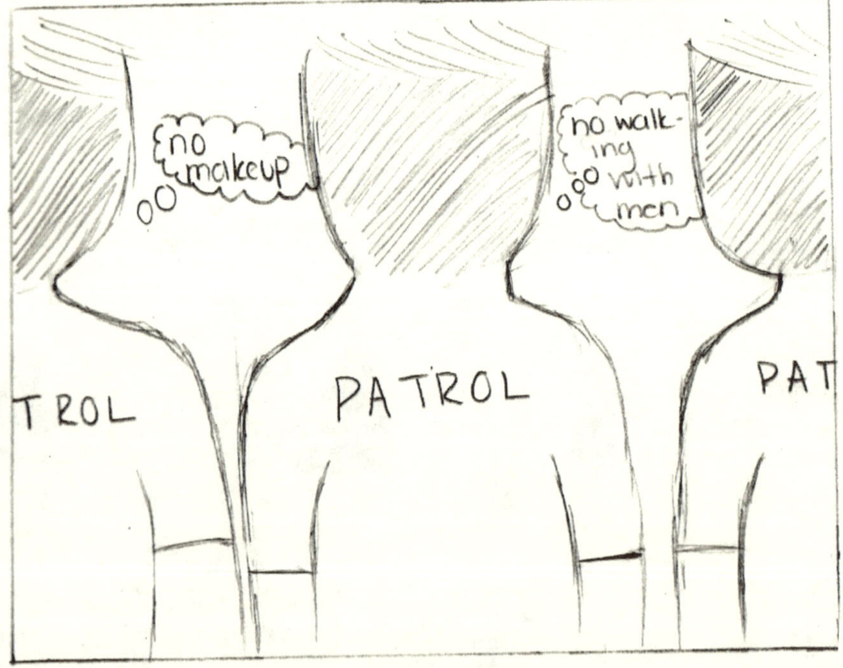

no makeup
no walking with men
TROL
PATROL
PAT

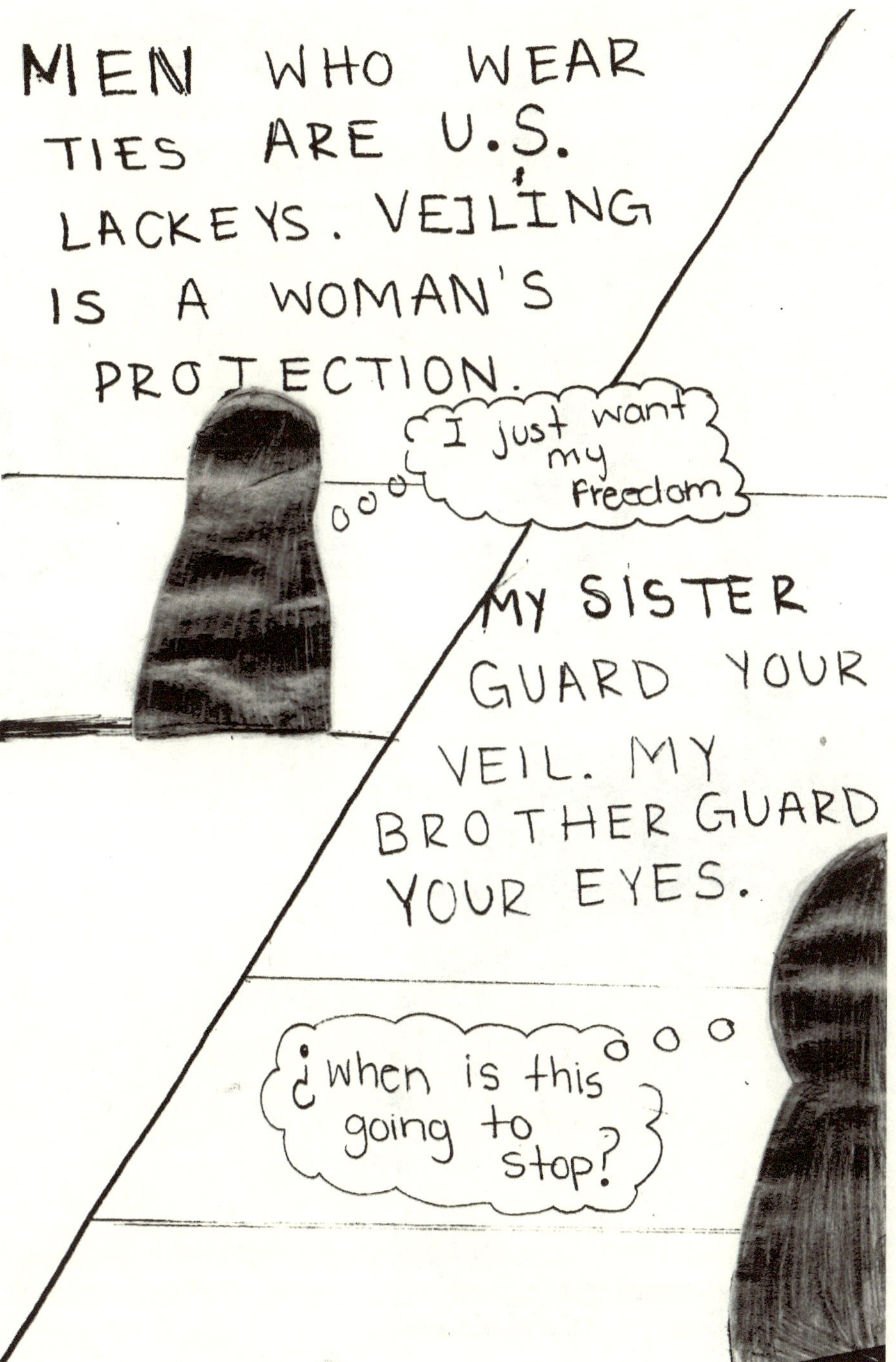
MEN WHO WEAR TIES ARE U.S. LACKEYS. VEILING IS A WOMAN'S PROTECTION.
I just want my freedom
MY SISTER GUARD YOUR VEIL. MY BROTHER GUARD YOUR EYES.
¿when is this going to stop?

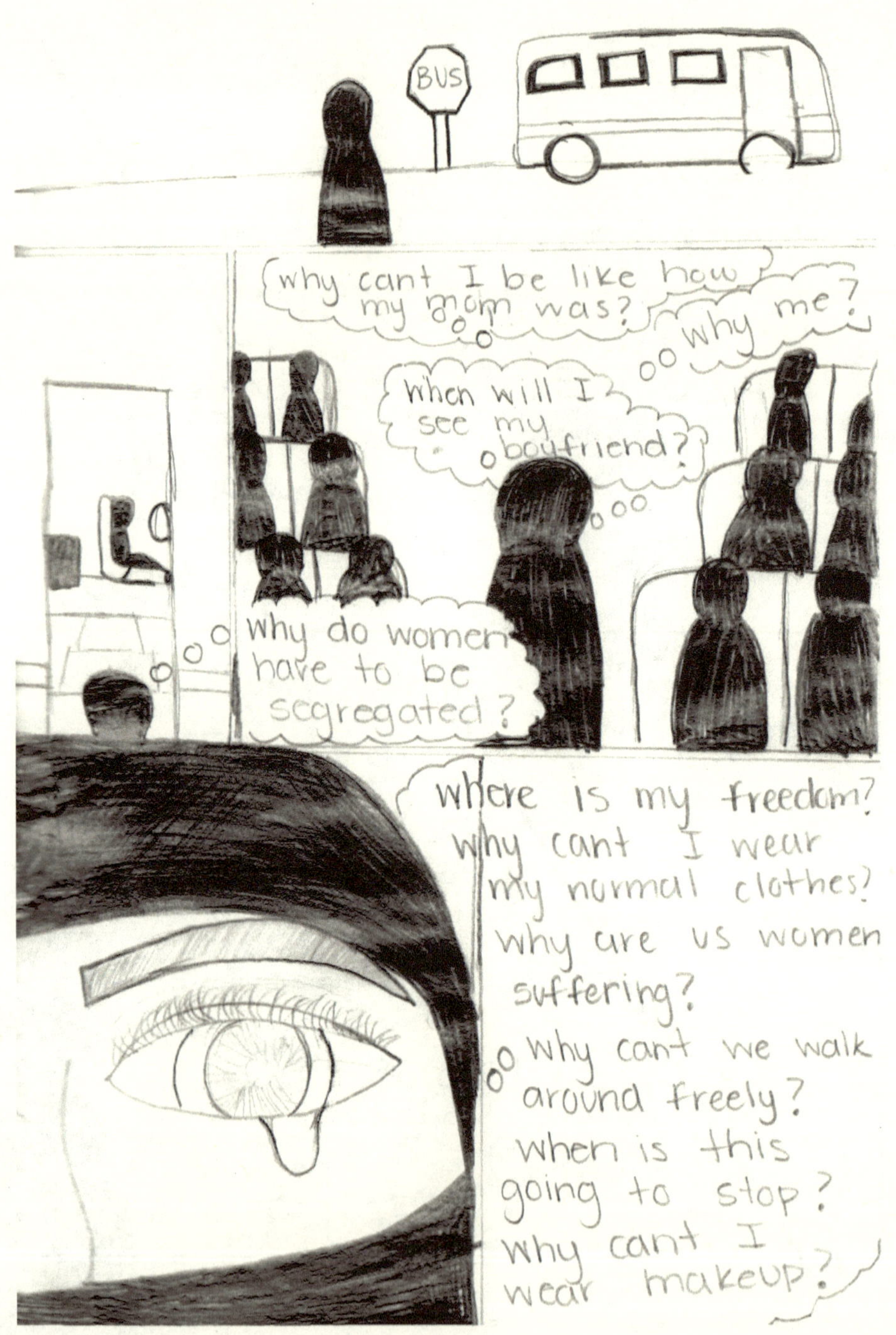
BUS
why cant I be like how my mom was?
why me?
When will I see my boyfriend?
why do women have to be segregated?
where is my freedom? why cant I wear my normal clothes? why are us women suffering? why cant we walk around freely? when is this going to stop? why cant I wear makeup?

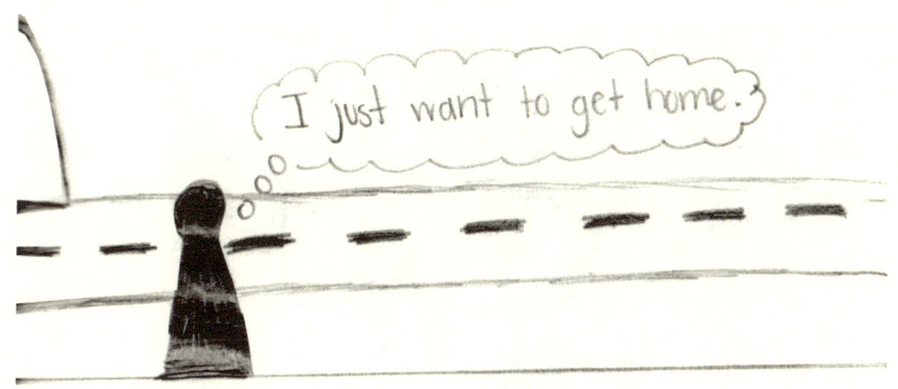

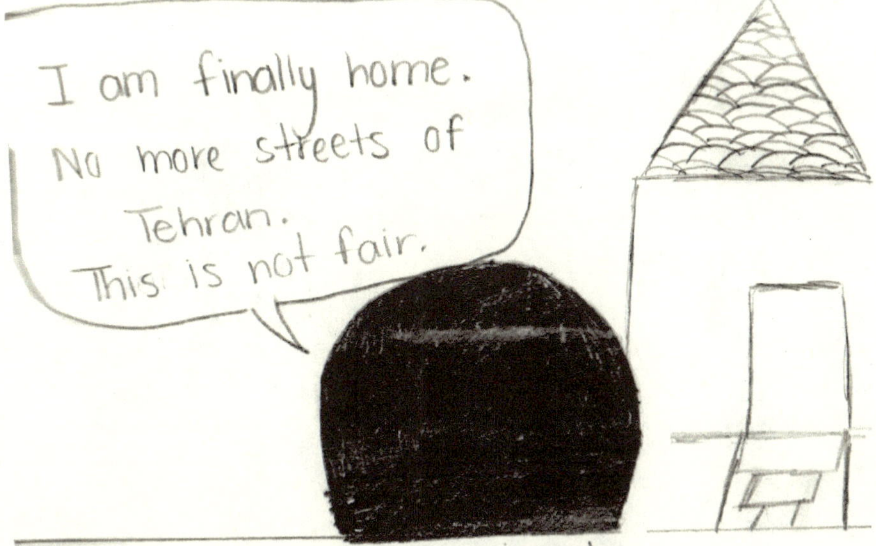

Sanaz is arriving to her house. She is over everything she went through on the streets of Tehran.

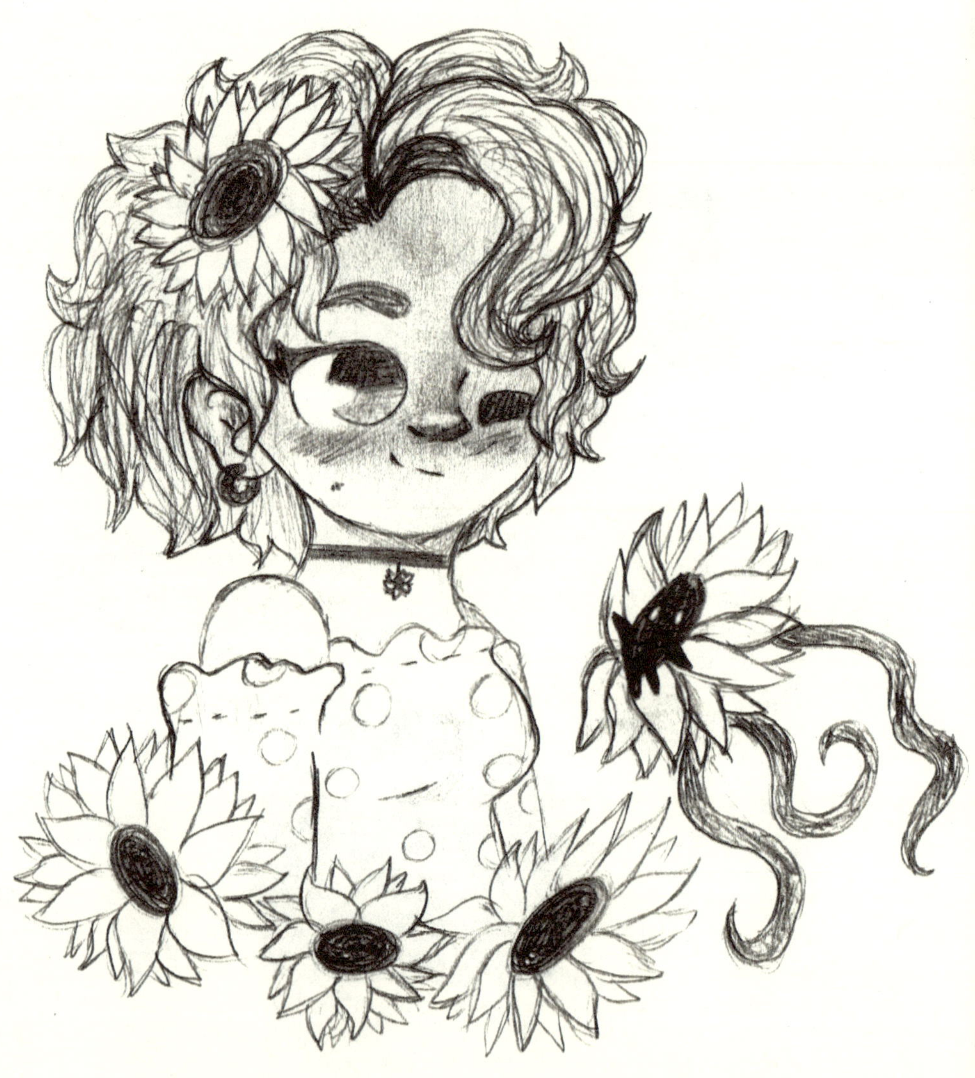

Teandra Johnson

8 Smells like Teen Shakespeare

Fear Of The Intruder

Karoline Blanco Chavez

Shall I go turn the lights on or to sleep?
I may wake up and not see life again,
Or I may fall asleep and it be deep.
Are the sounds outside my fear, or the rain?

I imagine the man covering me.
Not with his hands but with the black trash bag.
He locks me in the room, taking the key.
Then he goes around with the money bag.

My body is about to become numb.
My eyes are like the Niagara Falls.
The fear is taking over, I feel dumb.
Why do I feel trapped in my own fear walls?

My fear of the intruder lives with me,
And I hope that one day I will be free.

The Feeling of Getting Lost

Karoline Blanco Chavez

What will happen if I'm to disappear?
I wonder what it feels like to be gone.
At first, it may be a feeling of fear.
Then I come to realize that it's dawn.

No one has looked for me, am I forgot?
The feeling of being lost in the world
Has made me not want to be found or caught.
I feel like I am in the underworld.

It is hot, and I can´t be taken out.
I can not scream for help, I'm paralyzed.
There is no sound of lights, is it lights-out?
Do I really look like I am disguised?

No one seems to know where I am. I scream.
But then I remember it's all a dream.

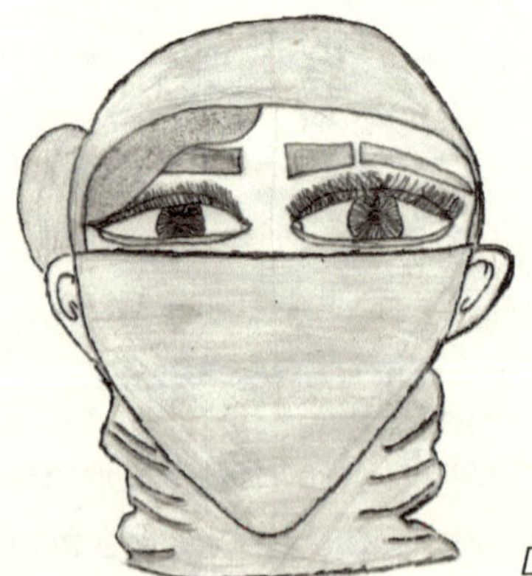

Da'Onna Watson

Count your Sheep

Liam Hansen

I may not go outside today hooray.
If it is true then it might make me sad.
I want happy. What about a buffet?
Then I can relax and have a good day.

I must stay inside and play all the games.
Although it may not be all that much wild.
At Least it is not so much of a fame.
It's better than being a too bored child.

What about country? Might go to a barn.
I must remember to set my clock right.
I might jump off, but to not break my arm.
Then I am ready to go walk a might.

For my fun is when I'm in bed to sleep.
For sleep is always when I count my sheep.

I'm Sick of COVID-19

Annabelle Lockridge

I'm sick and tired of COVID-19.
I just want life to go back to normal.
I hope this is all done by Halloween.
I'm ready to shop at the local mall.

This quarantine is driving me insane.
I want to see my friends at school so bad.
Social distance is only causing pain.
Isolation is making me go mad.

I miss everyone despite their antics.
I thought no school was really cool at first.
This virus now has me in a panic.
If this goes on any longer, I'll burst.

I so badly want this virus to end
So I can socialize and make new friends.

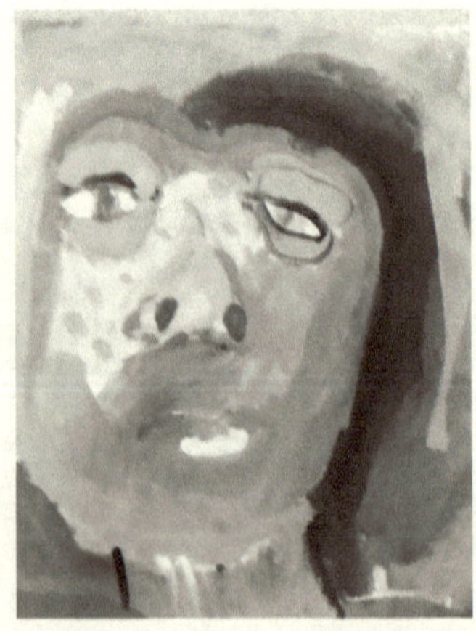

Thank You to My Family

Annabelle Lockridge

My family was here through bad and good.
We laugh, hangout, and fight, all day and night.
They make me feel welcome and understood.
They comfort me even when I'm not right.

They take us on beautiful vacations.
Where we will enjoy the scene together.
Due to this virus, I miss my cousins.
I wish it would end and all it's terror.

Just because I cherish my family,
Doesn't mean I want every day with them.
I wish this was just one big fantasy,
So we didn't have to deal with mayhem.

I can't wait for when we rejoin again.
Until then, I'll sit here tapping my pen.

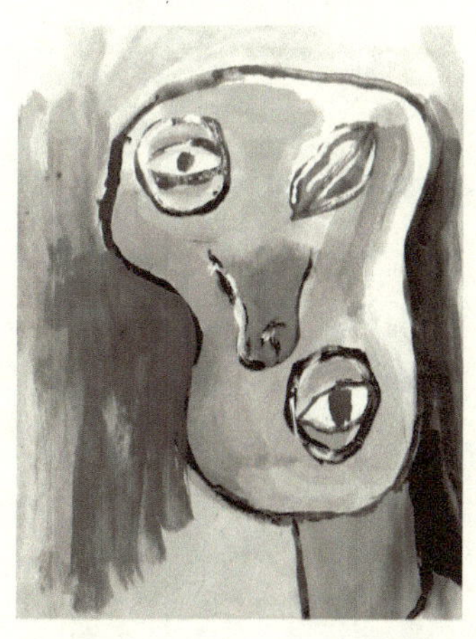

Mom

Edmirellys Merle

Mom, you have given me so much, thank you.
Always being there for me since day one.
Thanks for being there each and every year.
You have been my support to get it done.

You are a ray of sunshine in my life.
I appreciate all you do for me.
Thanks to you for giving me good advice.
Thanks for always being there for us three.

Mom you always are there when I need you.
Thank you for trying to be the best mom.
Thank you for helping me to get on through
All when I feel like an explosive bomb.

Thank you for always being my best friend.
Mom, you are always there until the end.

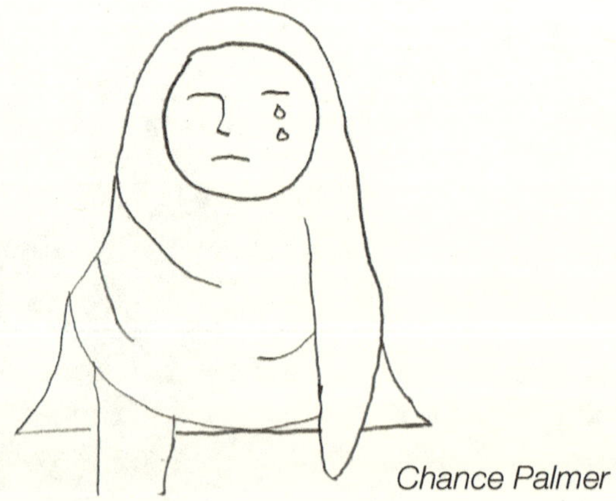

Chance Palmer

Bored

Riley Metz

We all want to go back to school so soon.
We are filled with boredom. Bring back fun, please.
Now we just stay asleep till late aft'noon.
We are waiting the day of hope release.

We all got stuck at home under orders.
Nobody is allowed to see friends. Sad.
The state has specific borders for us.
A lot of people are now going mad.

We are stuck at home 'lone, for good, for sure.
We miss human int'raction, but safely.
Our sadness will be hard to slowly cure.
We will all hopefully be free roam soon.

We crave the feels of being with the friends.
But we will leave everything to save ends.

The Unknown Simulation

Andrea Ramirez

It's like we are in a simulation.
It's one that humans can not get out of.
We can not find an end to persuasion.
We are all in a dimension above.

Manipulated into anything.
Everyone has no choice but to believe.
Soon enough we will forget everything,
So many things that could have been achieved.

Everything has been purposely provoked.
All of the lies have left everyone wrecked,
Being locked up left everyone unhoped.
Nobody knows when we will reconnect.

How long till the game is disconnected?
How long till every game is infected?

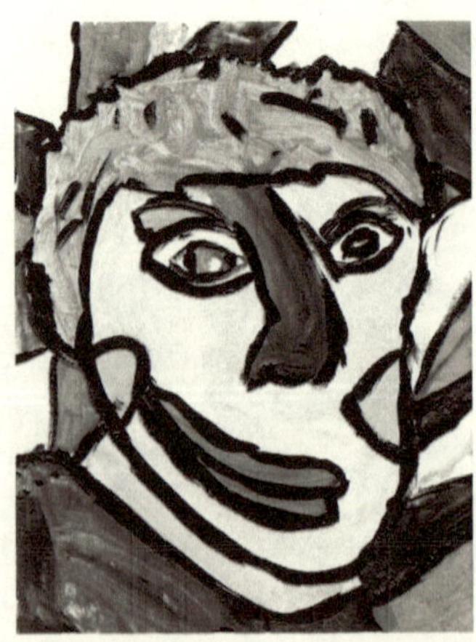

Underwater Paradise

Andrea Ramirez

Just close your eyes and enter the ocean,
You're alone in a small beautiful world.
It feels like you must have drunk a potion.
Let your body sway away and be held.

Let all your thoughts flow away with the breeze,
Let your imagination spread further.
Let the waves carry you away with ease,
Enter your new world and be the author.

Put yourself in a unique paradise,
One that you have never been in or seen.
A paradise you want to be in twice.
One you could not even see on a screen.

Then just live in that imagination,
Let your mind enjoy an exploration.

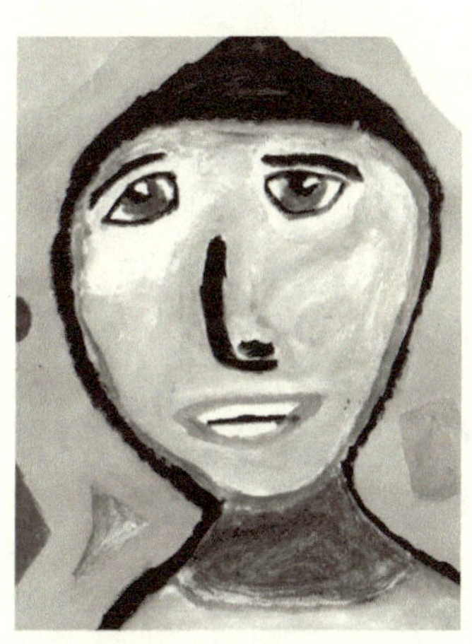

A Sonnet for Her

Ayden Sumaya-Beato

I lay awake at night thinking of her.
She is in my heart, my mind, and my dreams.
Thinking of her, my mind is but a blur,
Our love is fluid, much as if a stream.

Her eyes are beautiful like the night sky,
They hold my wishes when she looks at me.
I'm not always sweet, but for her, I try.
I'm no longer shackled. She makes me free.

I would do anything to see her smile.
I love how it makes her eyes almost close.
We've been dating for six months; that's a while,
She tames this beast like an enchanted rose.

Her hair is long, smooth, and so very blond.
I'm happy to have this amazing bond.

What Lousy Teachers

Alajah Thompson

What lousy teacher's parents can become.
They try their best to do things they cannot.
They teach us until they are unwelcome.
Having nothing to help on thee planet.

Days go past with our parents being here,
Try to teach us something that they don't know.
Figuring out the reading with Shakespeare.
Sticking to the talking about rainbows.

Days we learn about every subject there.
Loads and loads of work that we have to do.
Believing they need to stick to child care.
This is going to be hard to get on through.

What lousy teacher's parents can become.
These are the things that I need to escape from.

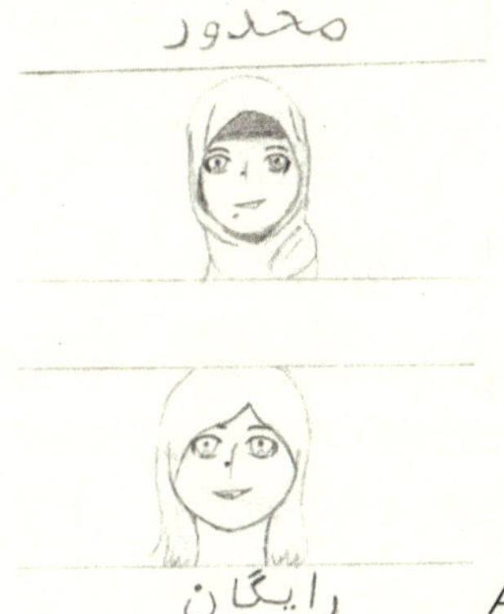

Ayden Sumaya-Beato

Furious

Alajah Thompson

COVID-19 is really serious.
Having no school to attend to at all.
This is making everyone furious.
We can't even go to the effing mall.

Having to do school work each day, all day;
It's kind of getting annoying real fast.
Starting to get boring and start to gray.
We really hope this thing is of the past.

Having to make bonds with the other ones,
While trying to get along with people.
With things that come, other things will soon come.
They're trying with the business people.

With the COVID-19 being so bad,
We really want to have what we once had.

Discover

Da'Onna Watson

A young girl who cannot chase all her dreams,
Oh how the best dreams are hard to uncov'r!
In her sleep her dreams are not as it seems,
If the girl finds it hard to discover.

Shall the young girl search for the dreams she seeks?
Those of which are near loss and extinction.
When she finds the dreams she'll take a peek
At how her truths and lies show distinction.

As her thoughts race around her heavy mind,
She dreams, a vivid dream, thou art so vile.
Insects flying around! Are these dreams kind?
Shall she bask thy dream? Does she like thy style?

Thus being said, her dream is essential,
It documents her life and potential.

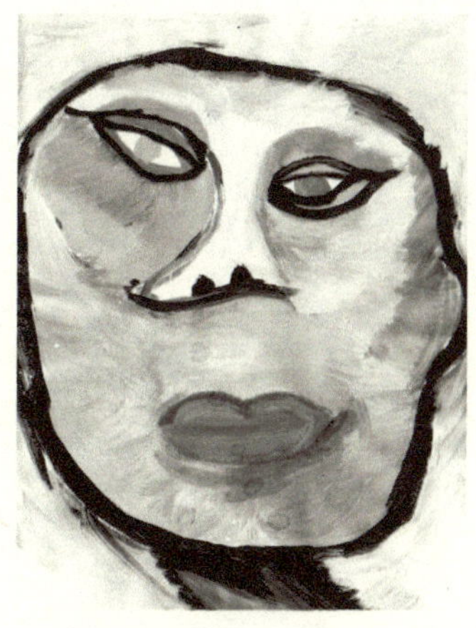

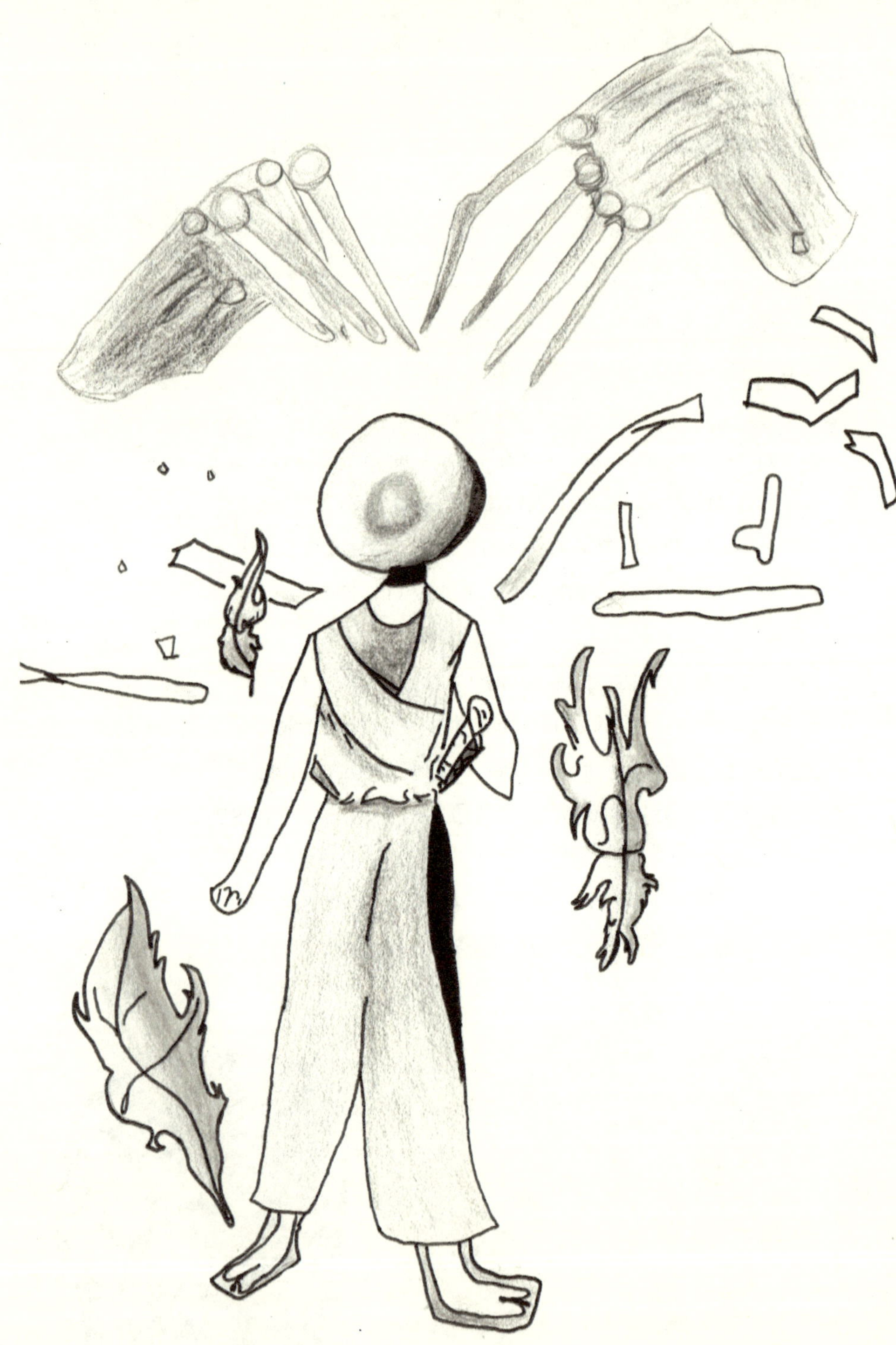

Olivia Sumerlin

9 Pandemic Panic

Bye School and Hello Home

Erick Hidalgo

Is it me or is it you or is the world gone wrong?
This strange feeling of gone,
Like the world is falling apart.
What do we do and what do we say?

This is a strange place and a strange feeling,
We are fine and let's get along,
Or are we now?
Let's find out.

This world is a mess.
We take and we go.
We think we are also bold,
Yet no one is home.

Lions in a Cage

Karoline Blanco

Children have no school, wondering when
They will be able to see their friends.
Little kids have no fun, wondering when
They can go back outside and play.
Some people have become the lion in a cage.
They can not get out, they are trapped.

People say it is all exaggerated, but people are dying.
What if it is a message from God for need of change?
What if it is our punishment for all the bad we have done?
It was all fun at first, hearing these stories, but
COVID-19 is what we all fear now.

People in public are wearing medical masks for protection.
People in public are wearing blue latex gloves for protection.
People stay feet away from each other for protection.
People have turned on each other,
Fighting over things that were once unnecessary.
What if there is no end?

Earth

Yessica Morales

Earth isn't safe.
Earth is sick.
Earth doesn't want us to be bad and do bad things.
Our planet isn't safe.

Being locked in feels like begin in prison.
No going outside.
Just eating, sleeping and finding out what to do.
Earth is ending.

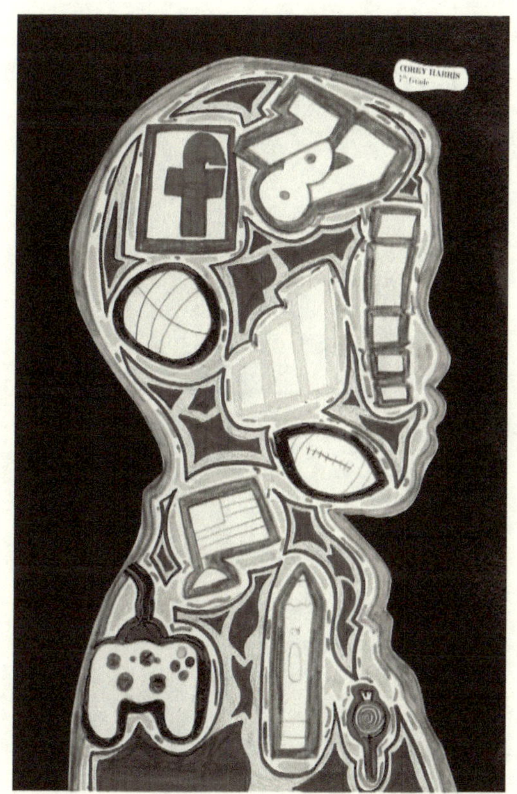

Schools is Shut Down

Erick Hidalgo

That's it, we're done for.
Not just school but stores.
Are our homes next?
Maybe or maybe not.

We must protect ourselves,
And our families at least.
We must not cry,
But fight for this last time.

We will win this fight.
We have faced worse.
Today is not the day to give up.
Life will be normal again.

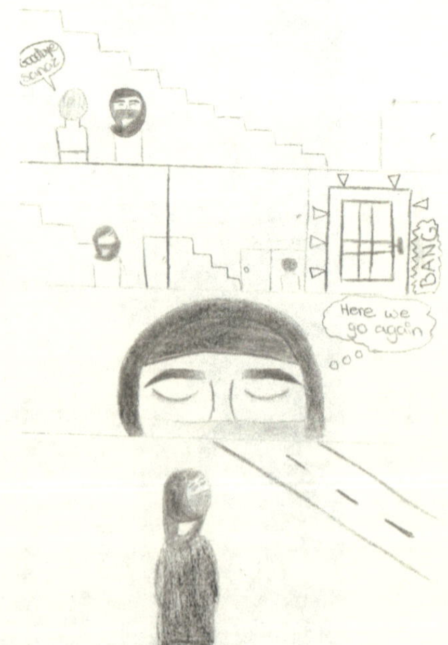

Danna Texis

Social Distancing

Annabelle Lockridge

Stay home you people! Stay away from me!
This virus is serious for you and for me.
Things aren't being cancelled for "No stinkin' reason."
This is more serious than our yearly flu season.

Scientist, doctors, and all those other things
Have told us to practice social distancing.
I know it feels like your at home in a coop,
But please people! 6 feet apart from each group.

Don't worry about boredom, there's many things to do.
Go for a walk on the dock, sit alone on your canoe.
Stay away from big crowds and stay away from me!
Please! Oh! Please people! Practice social distancing!

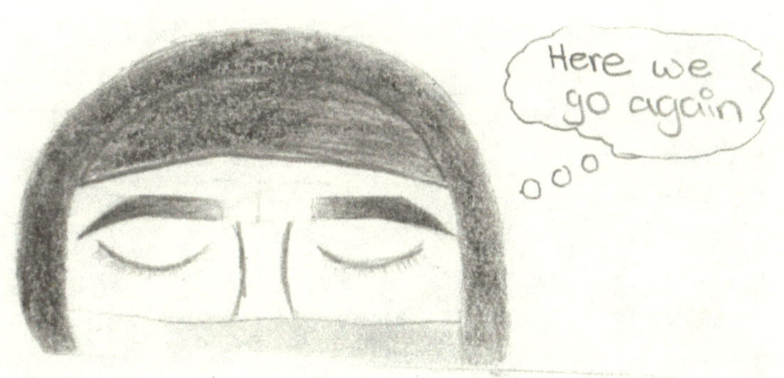

Danna Texis

Oh No!

Yessica Morales

Oh no, here we go again.
Another day of no school
And just staying home.

Another day of doing nothing but sleeping
And doing school work since
School died.
All we want is to be free and not just stay home.

Our freedom has died, society has died, being
In public has died, mostly our lives are ruined.

Everybody wants to be free
And not locked in
Their homes.
All we want is freedom.

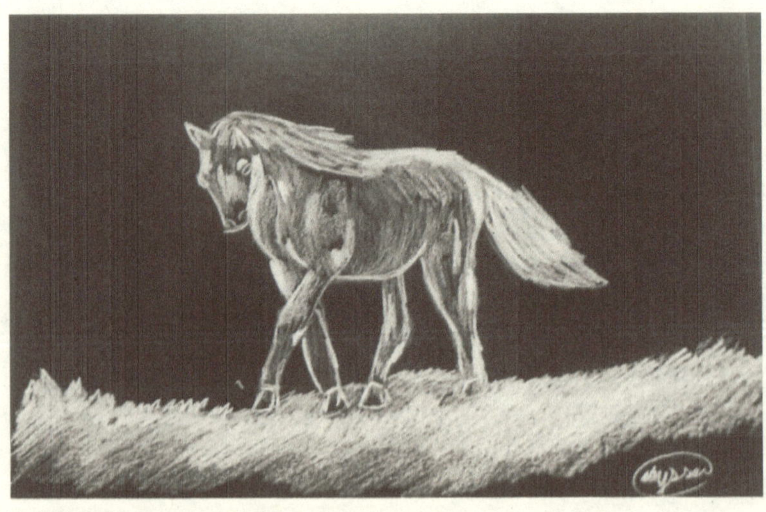

Here's a Lot of Whining

Victor Santamaria

Life sucks, school sucks, everything sucks now.
You can't go anywhere, everywhere just sucks.
McDonalds doesn't enlighten our days anymore,
And Starbucks is just boring coffee.

I can't go to Chuck E. Cheese,
Frankie's Fun Park, or Carowinds.
I can't go anywhere to have fun
Or do something fun.
This isn't fair.

I hate not getting to play my sports or
Having fun with my friends like I used to do.
Right now I would probably be on a bus
Going to my soccer game.
That would have me hyped up.

I feel very sad and broken because of this outbreak.
It really did take a lot of things away from me and all of us,
But all we can do to make it
End quicker is to do nothing and stay home.
So I advise all of us to stay home and do nothing,
Because you are the reason for it.

The New Unnormal

Yessica Morales

I wake up.
I get ready.
We go to the store.
There's nobody.
No toilet paper, no water.
Is the world ending?
Are my friends saying the truth?
The world is ending.
We leave the store with only groceries.
The drive back is weird.
No traffic, no slow cars, no honking.
The world is ending.

You Are Now Gone

Brandon Hernandez

You are now gone.
Disappeared into the night.
I have no life.

Just like that,
My fingers snap.
Will you be back?

I'm trapped.
No way out.
It's hard to breathe.

What to do now?
We all have frowns.
It's a ghost town.

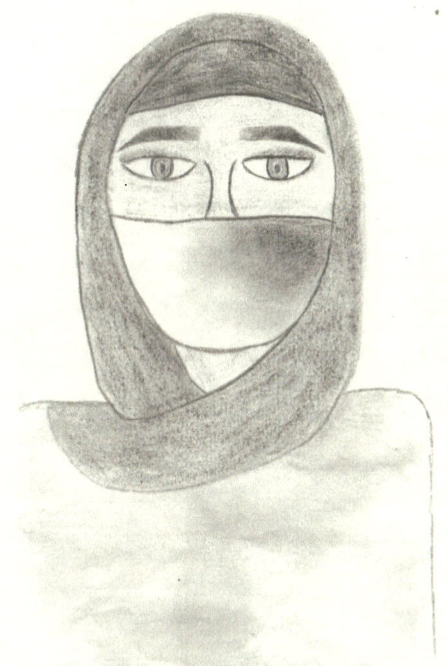

Danna Texis

I Wanted to Work and Other Lies

Victor Santamaria

School has died sadly.
It breaks my heart that it has left me.
Now I can't stay up till 1am to do work.
That totally sucks man, I really wanted to work.

My teachers' spirits have died as well.
That totally sucks for us,
Because we wanted to work.
I honor their hard working methods,
But they should take a rest.
So sad my teachers won't be my regular teachers again.
No more yelling and being told what to do,
That is very heartbreaking to me.

When I imagine being at home,
Doing nothing but work, it sucks.
My school spirit has died off, like a dying Christmas tree.
I am sooo sad that things had to end like this.
And I hope things will be
Back to normal sooner or later.

Stay in a Book

Ja'Lea Anderson

Coronavirus is really changing our lives.
Things aren't the same. People are acting
Different. There people who care a lot, and
There are people who're acting like it's nothing.

We can't really do nothing anymore. Like it's like
The whole world is shut done except a few things.
But it is now that I think about it. We can't do anything
Can't really even go out. Can't be in big crowds.

We just have to be alone.
We have to stay put. Us kids should just stay in a book.
There's a lot of things different and
There are a lot of things that are the same.

We all need to stay safe.

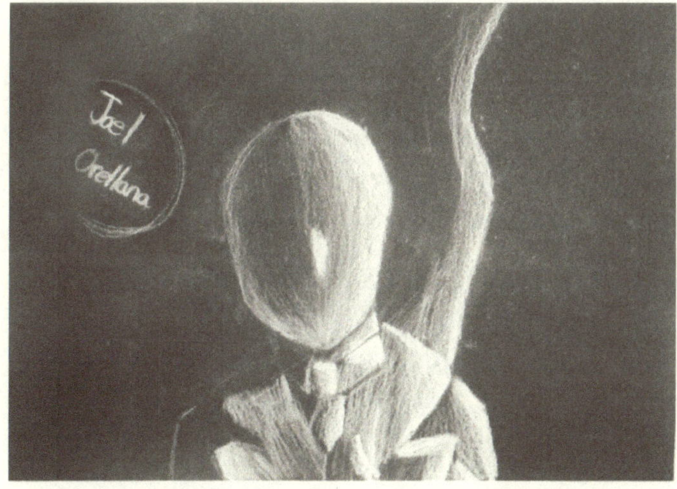

Values Have Died

Karoline Blanco

Values have died.
Half of us don't value our parents.
Some of us do.
Not until our parents are gone
And start saying boo.
Yeap they die.

This isn't a fairytale or a joke.
You can even ask a pope.
You better grab your friend.
Oh well, it is the end.

What if God is just mad at us
And is making us suffer?
What if there is no God,
And the bible and everything is a lie?
Meanwhile, your parents are dead,
And their values are, too.

2020 is a Movie

Karoline Blanco

People said 2020 was going to be a movie.
Maybe it was called, "The End of the World."
Remember that movie called "Five Feet Apart?"
We are living in it.

Remember how they predicted
"2020 will have flying cars?"
They meant flying helicopters saving our nation.
We are trapped with nowhere to go.
Our lives are now a computer screen,
Or a living room view.

Over 300,000 dying, and
Hand sanitizer is going to save us?
They say it's just old people, but young people
Have become the next target.
Remember what it was like,
Being able to go to a store
And buy anything?

Just remember.

2020 is becoming the movie,
"The End of the World,"
But this is just the first 10 minutes.

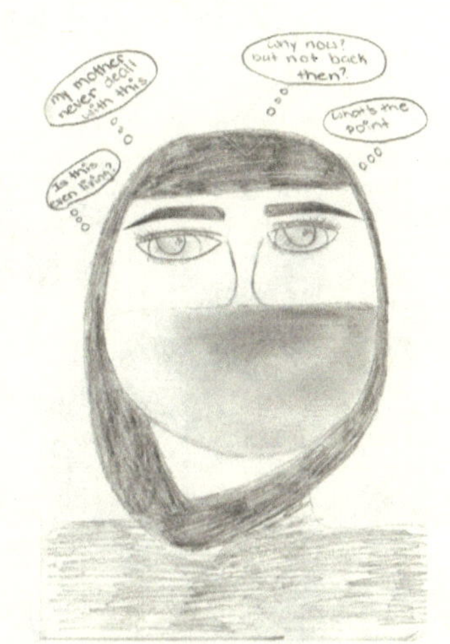

Danna Texis

Fade to Sleep

Tanaysha Chappell

Ruined and buried deep,
Our life as humans fades to sleep
As everything in life dies.

My food supply has run dry.
Stores are closing one by one,
And food is becoming scarce.

Doors are locked and roads are clear.
Socialites stay at home and weep.
Kids relax and play games and school is still here.

Doing work to pass the time as quarantine is boring.
Nothing can compete as coronavirus is still a warning.
All I do is stay at home and sleep,
Hoping that soon this pandemic will be done.

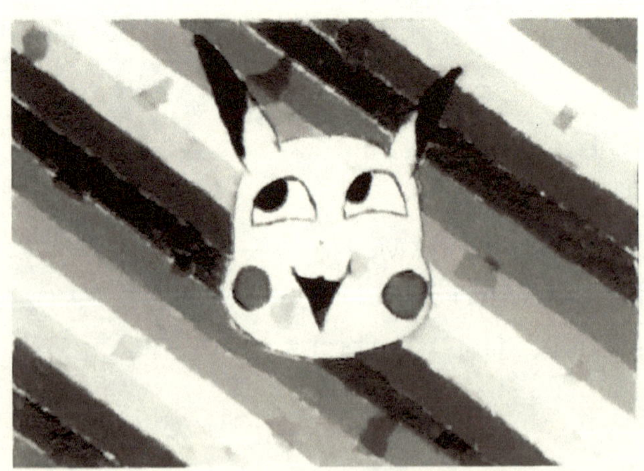

COVID-19

Shekynah Moore

If there is a reason for this, it needs to be explained.
Why does every day start the same and end the same?
I do nothing but sit and complain and waste time.
Time is of the essence.
Not anymore.

Now we have to keep score of the people
Who are dying for no reason,
And the people who scroll their phones not caring, or
Caring way too much.
Those people who live in fear of an invisible monster.
Not the invisible man, but the coronavirus.

COVID-19.
This monster dominates our nations
Yet cures the world that we made
Sick since man first made weapons.
It's a hitman, but also a savior to the world
And to humanity.

Always Empty

Tanaysha Chappell

The stores are always empty in one section or two.
It's hard to find things you need and
They put a limit on it, too.
Everytime they restock there is always another horde.
You think that you will find something,
So you go to many stores.

But it is always disappointing
When you find no soap bars.
Realizing that the pandemic is coming,
You have all the cleaning supplies,
But food is what you are missing.

You drive around to stores and there is limited food,
And fast food only uses drive thrus.
As you start to go home, you realize
How bored you are going to be.

You have no friends, and rely on your phone and tv.
You don't have work, but you still have to pay the bills.
And you're running out of fuel for your car
As you struggle to find a job.

Our Way of Life is Dead

Annabelle Lockridge

Our way of life is dead.
Normal has shriveled up and died.
Our routines have been thrown into
A giant garbage bin and burned.
Everything is different and will never be the same.

My sister should be in Americorps, enjoying California.
My mom should be at work, taking care of her kids.
My brother and I should be at school,
Having fun with our friends.

Our way of life is dead.
It has been shattered, stomped on, and broke.
I should be somewhere else completely.
This is not normal and it never will be.

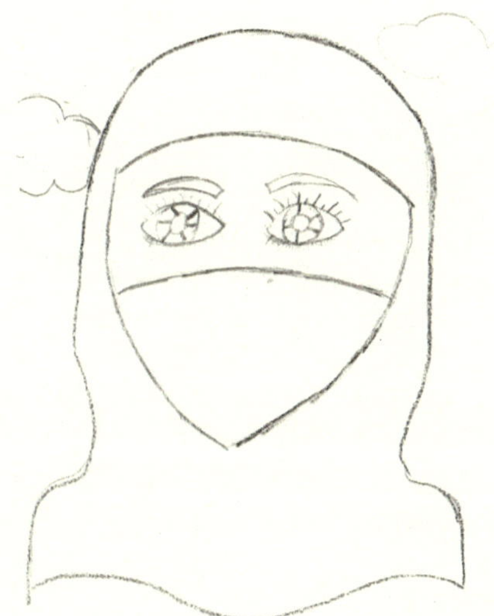

Maireini Cano Cano

Our New Life

Riley Metz

Our freedom is revoked.
We cannot leave our house.
No more going to the movies,
No more going to Target to hang out with friends.

Our freedom is revoked.
No more seeing our friends,
No more gossiping in the school bathrooms.

Our freedom is revoked.
We all want everything back to normal.
We want to go back to school and socialize.
We want our lives back.

These Chaotic Days

Bradley Perez

Stressing about these random things.
Nothing I had to worry about before.
Now I'm slowly going insane,
Forgetting what day it is,
Yet keeping track of time.
Work that's due in an hour.
Now I'm rushing to do everything,
Wondering how everyone else is doing.

Am I being left behind?
A lot of questions
Flood into my head.

What day is it again?

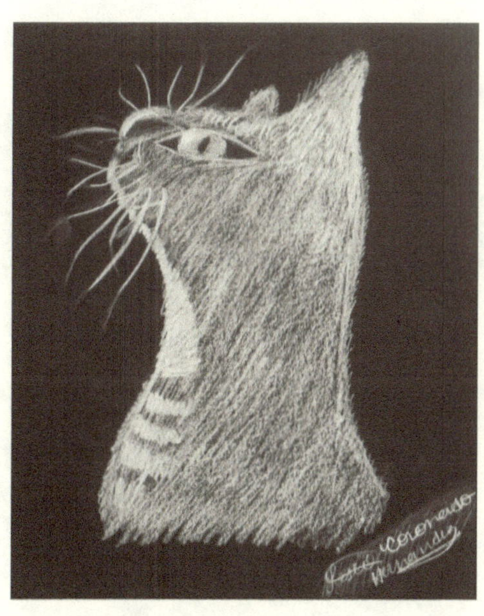

Emotions

Riley Metz

It all happened so suddenly.
The weekend turned into a long vacation.
We did not get to say a final goodbye to anyone.

School after school,
Restaurant after restaurant,
Store after store
All closed in an instant.

So many people left devastated.
People losing their jobs,
Many not making money,
The government is falling apart.

Everybody is devastated.

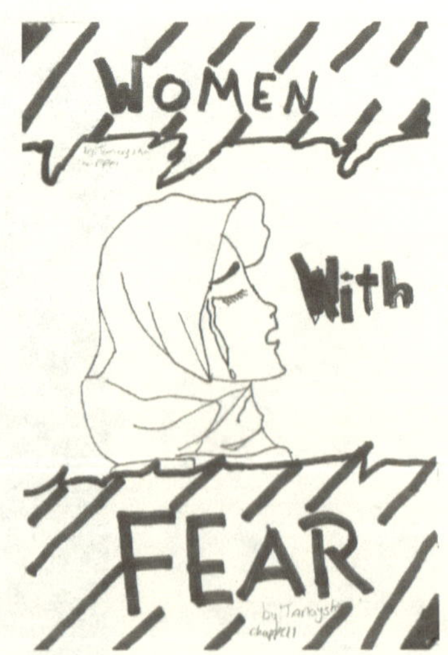

Tanaysha Chappell

Another Light

Shekynah Moore

I'll see you in another light.
I'll see you when these times die down.
I'll see you smiling in a different crowd.
Too bad we will never be in a crowd.

Good-bye, life as we knew it.
I know you're probably having the time of your life at a rave.
A rave of forgetting and turmoil.
Maybe I'll see you in another light.

What other light could I see you in?
How will I see you?
Where will I see you?
Maybe never, maybe soon, maybe later.

My Fear

Ayden Sumaya-Beato

I fear the unknown; the kind I haven't seen.
This is a new situation I've never been in.
The fear for my family in Florida,
The fear for my family in the Philippines.

This is all too much.
I lay awake like an insomniac,
Thinking of what could happen.
I know so little, but fear so much.

I have barricaded myself in the house,
Only leaving to get groceries or things that I need.
Laying down or playing video games,
To distract myself from this fear.

This is my fear.

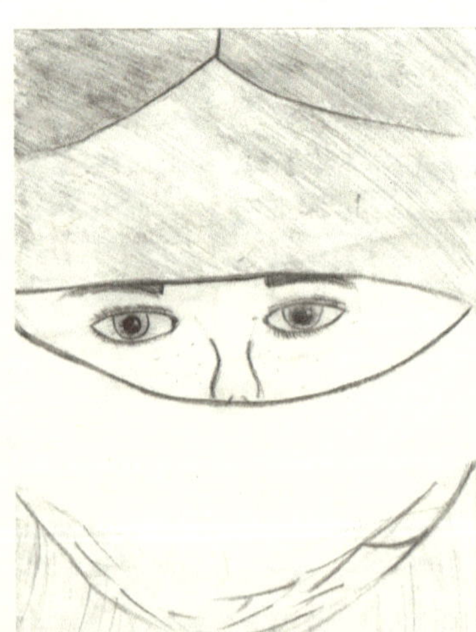

Andrea Ramirez

What are We?

Jose Ortiz

The crisis is something new or recent.
New may mean better for some people.
This is something unexpected
Which many will catch by surprise.

This is somewhat true.
New is not always better,
But we were caught by surprise.
However, how did this change how people live?

As we have seen, this has changed people a lot.
This is like a never-ending Black Friday.
First they here about the virus,
Which is like the deals that are going on,
Then they all fight over the supplies.
The next thing you know the stores are empty.

What is this?
What is going through people's heads?
Do they care about the others or just themselves?
This makes me think of people in a different light.

Are we this miserable?
Are we this greedy?
Or what are we?

Think about it.

The Place

Bradley Perez

Going to a place
I find safe.
Smiling at the things others say.
This place is now empty.

Wondering if it'll open soon
So I can let out a breath of relief.
Continue to do the work
That keeps me alive.

Slowly it starts to fade away.
The picture I last remember,
The people I laugh with,
It's all becoming a blur.

Remembering the days I yearned for the bell.
Wanting to just say goodbye.
Now I hate what I said,
But I want to go back to this weird place.

The Death of My Freedom

Ayden Sumaya-Beato

I want to see my friends and family but cannot.
I want to go to the park but cannot.
I want to take my Spring Break trip to Florida but cannot,
Because you, my freedom, are dead.

I want to leave this house but cannot.
I look out the window, knowing that I cannot.
For once I want to go shopping to
Find clothes that fit but cannot,
Because you, my freedom, are dead.

To the freedom to move freely, I say farewell.
To the freedom of seeing my family in Florida, I say farewell.
To the plans I have made, I say farewell,
Because you, my freedom, are dead.

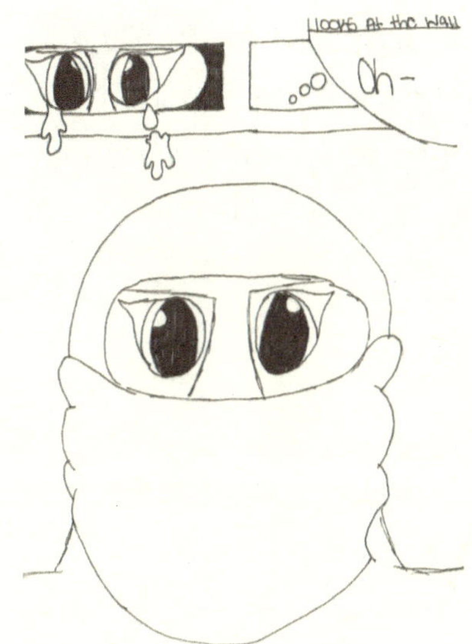

Alajah Thompson

Toilet Paper

Ayden Sumaya-Beato

Toilet paper, please.
It is getting hard to find.
Gee, thanks, Corona.

I Really Want to...

I really want to go to the beach,
I'd even settle for the pool on base.
I really want to go swimming,
But, no, I'm stuck wanting.

I really want to hang out with my girlfriend at the movies.
I'd even settle for swinging at the park.
I really want to see her,
But, no, I'm stuck wanting.

I really want to go visit my family in Florida,
I'd even settle for them coming here for a weekend.
I really want to see them in person.
But, no, I'm stuck wanting.

They Need to Find a Cure

Joshua Hernandez

Our freedom has been taken by this virus.
Forced to be huddled down in our homes,
Wondering when we can go
Back outside and socialize with friends.

The news stresses everyone out by
Making things more exaggerated.
People are wondering when a
Cure for this virus will appear.

Thousands could be saved if a cure comes out,
But who knows if there ever will be a cure.
I wonder when I can see my friends,
Praying every night that this just goes away

So I don't get a needle shot.
Doctors working hard to find a cure,
Just wanting to go home and see their families,
But can't because they need to find a cure.

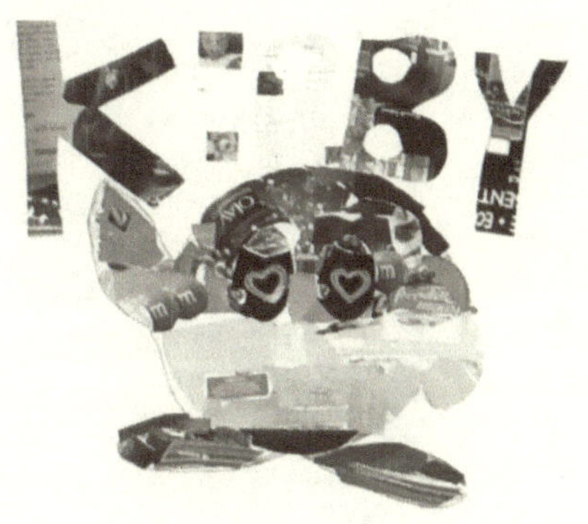

My 8th Grade Year Elegy

Chance Palmer

Rest In Peace, 8th grade year.
Locked in a house
With challenging work,
This virus is worse than the plague.

Every day,
Children across the world did not want to go to school.
Next thing ya know,
"School has been cancelled."

We all deep down miss school.
We were supposed to walk down
To our next stage of life,
And now we may not.

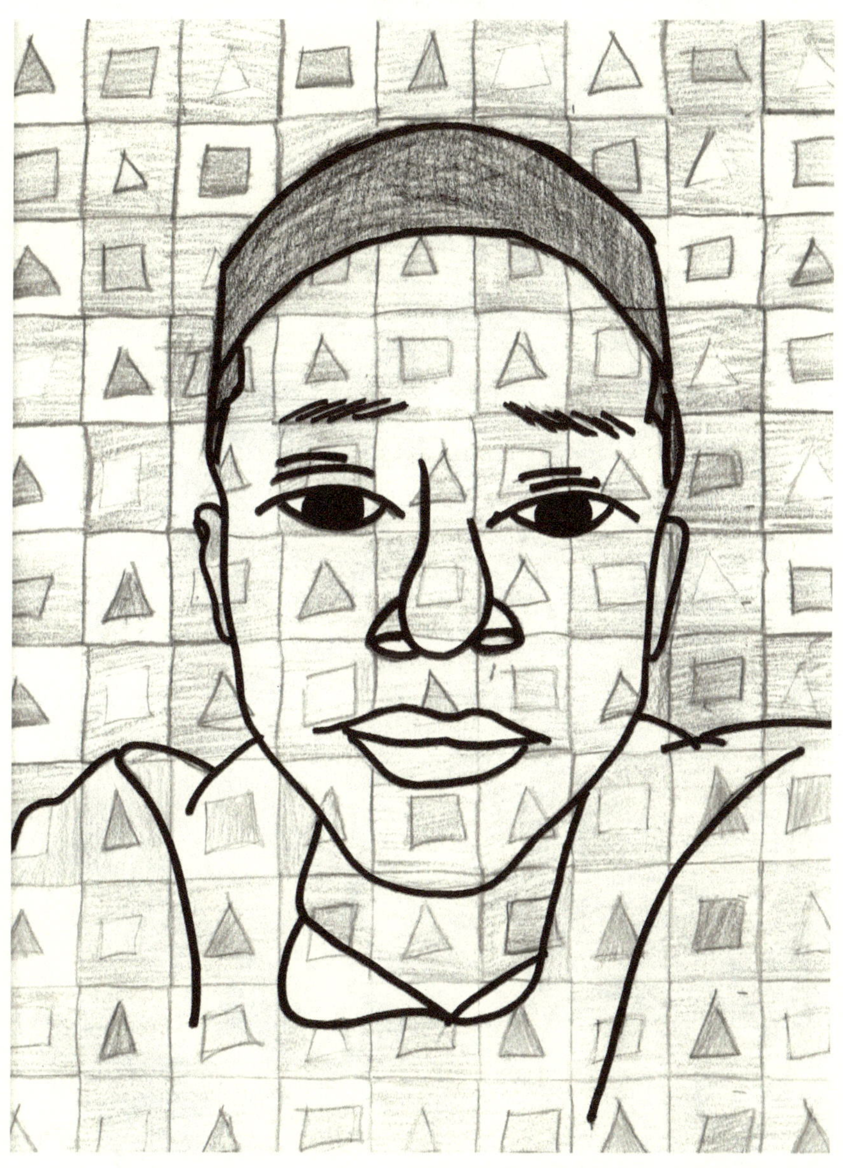

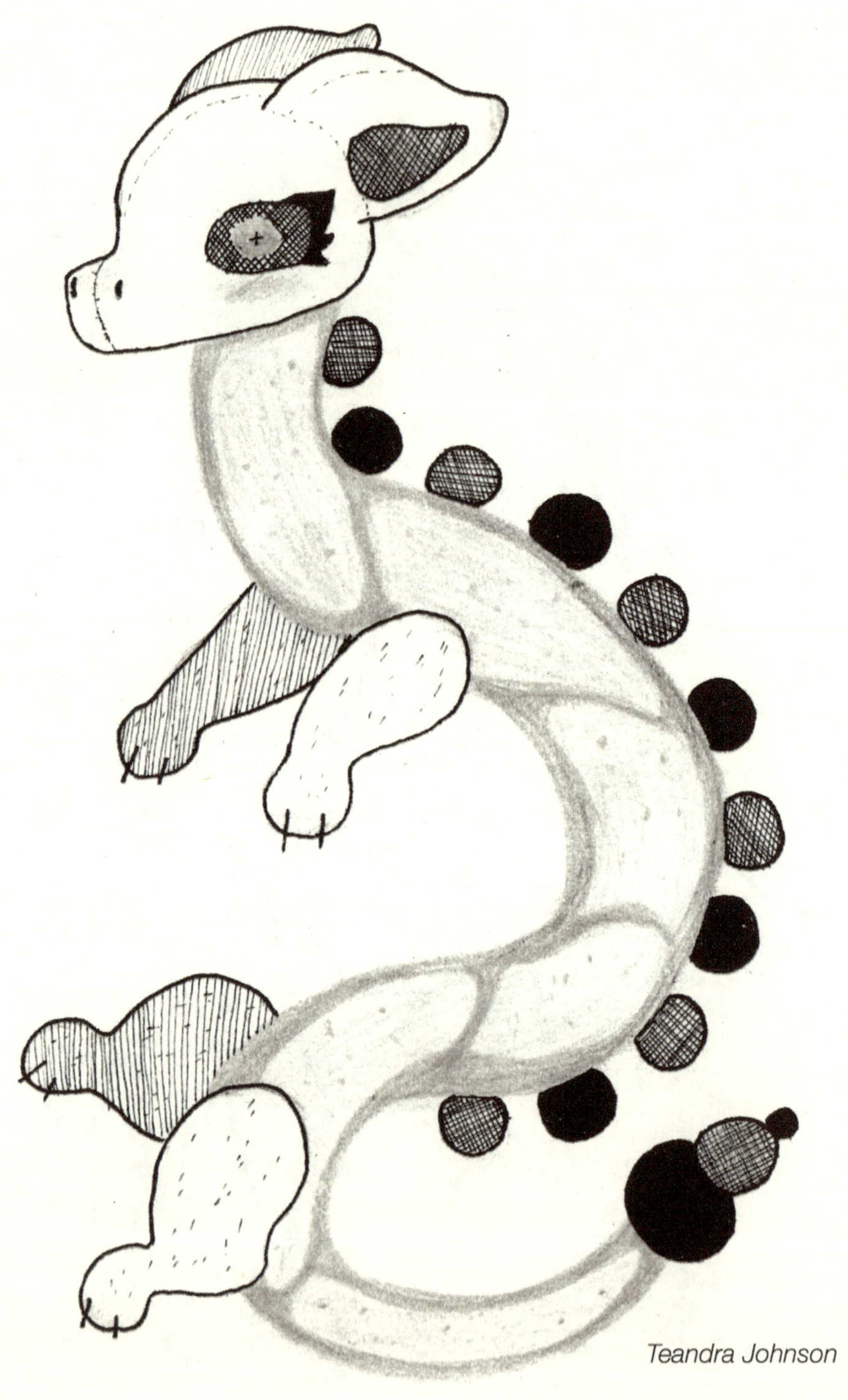

Teandra Johnson

10 Deep Rhetoric

Be Smart!

Ayden Sumaya-Beato

Things that I think are wise,
Apart from the obvious....old guys,
Would be to think about the needs,
Of all of our societies.

Don't you think that it would be smart,
To stay indoors?...Work on art!
There's tons of things that we could all do,
To make this easier and faster to get through.

Use not only your heart, but also your head.
Stay indoors, lay in bed.
Whatever it is that you choose to do,
Think about it, is it helping people other than you?

132 Suicides

Karoline Blanco

The 132 suicides per day have been the
Saddest parts of our world.
Suicide has become deadly amongst most teens.
Death is the answer amongst most.
These people think death is the key to happiness.

Why is it most common amongst women?
Why is it more common for them to think these things?
Over 100,000 people die a year,
And it has become a world problem.

When will suicide not exist to these people?
When the thoughts go away,
These people will still live in sadness.
Is suicide what most people think of?
The feeling of sadness develops the thoughts of suicide,
As well as trauma and abuse.

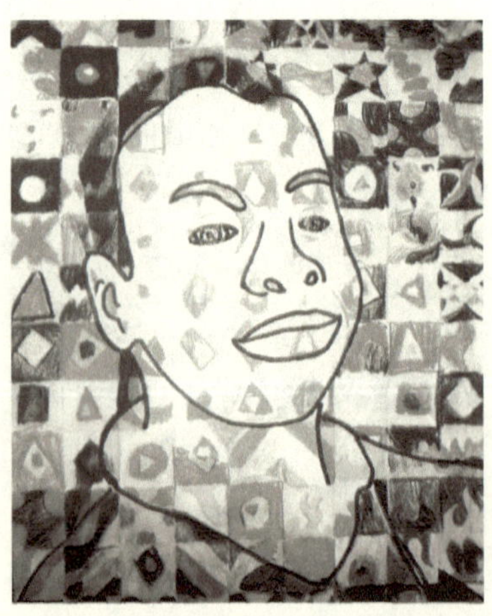

If I Don't Get In

Annabelle Lockridge

I start to panic.
I tell myself to take deep breaths
Because, no matter what,
I'll be alright.
Terrifying scenarios fill my head
With fear and dread.

I can't picture myself anywhere else
Besides this school.
I doubt they would want me.
I am not smart enough or strong enough.
I am not good enough.

Tears flooding my eyes and dripping down my face.
It's just a stupid school and I am overreacting.
No matter how hard I try, I can't decline the thought
Of me not getting in.

5 out of 5 Times

Karoline Blanco

Being a child in a world full of hate, I once experienced it.
I watch the news and see what our world has turned into.
5 out of 5 times, violence is shown on television.
How did we get to this point?
I see stories on children,
Killed and injured for trying to live in this world.
I see stories everyday.

Have you heard about the boy that was killed?
Because I have.

Have you seen how violent our world has become?
Because I have.

Have you heard about the girl that was killed?
Because I have.

We all hear stories, but I have seen them.
Imagine knowing that our world has one less life,
Because I know that it has happened.
I know it will happen, because one day.
One day there will be no one left.

Great Grandma Nelson

Annabelle Lockridge

She is on the verge of death.
She's 97 and counting.
Even though she is the strongest woman I know,
Her chances are low.

People 65 or older accounted for 80% of the deaths from COVID-19
Will she be a part of that percent?
Will I get to say goodbye?
Was it already her time?

She is weak, but continues to act strong.
The average age to die in the US is 78.69 years old.
She is nearly two decades past that.
She told me she wanted to die,
But I'm not ready to say goodbye.

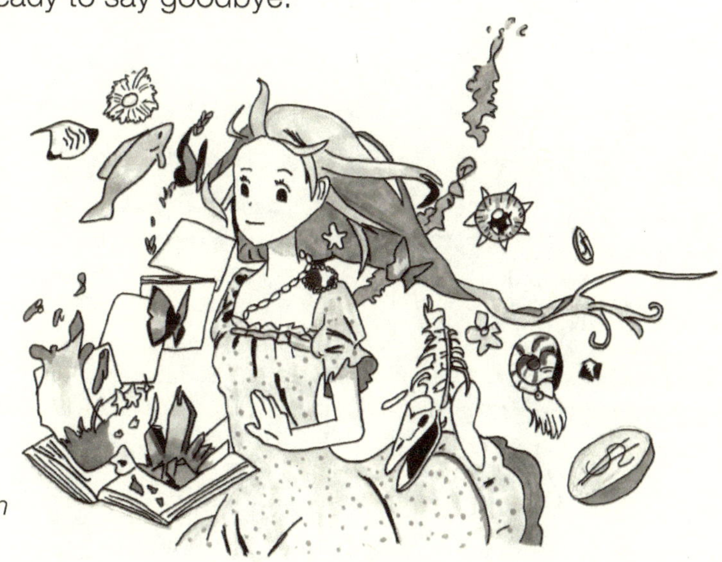

Olivia Summerlin

Deep Thoughts

Andrea Ramirez

Is getting help a good choice?
Or do you just take the easier route and end it?
Maybe it is worth doing it.
If a person does not want help,
They are most likely going to end it the easier way…

Through death.

People die from depression from around 60%.
Each time a person goes around depression
There is always a chance of death.
People often try to seek help
But it does not get the help needed.
Families constantly lose loved ones from this.
All they are able to do is be there
Everyday for every step of the way.

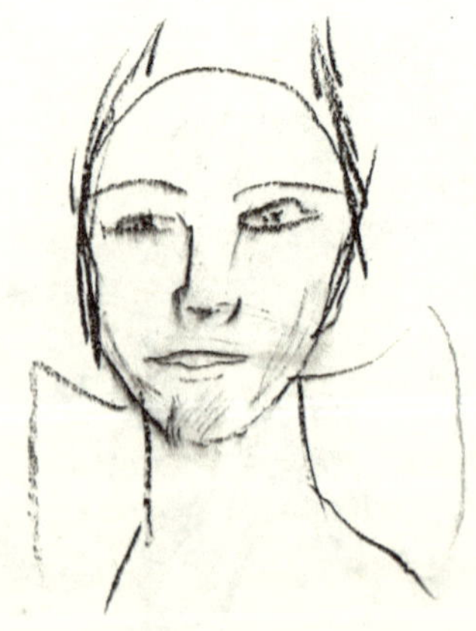

I know that from experience.
Imagine seeing a loved one locked up in the room,
But you know that is not like them.
Them not even wanting to talk to you or hang out with you.
It is one of the worst feelings because that makes you think.

Did I do something wrong? Am I not good enough?
Am I just a terrible person? What can I do now?

Having to think all of those things and then also
Knowing that there is a chance of death
Hurts more than most things.
Thinking that you lost someone because
You could not help them.
The truth is just be there for them,
And hope for the best.

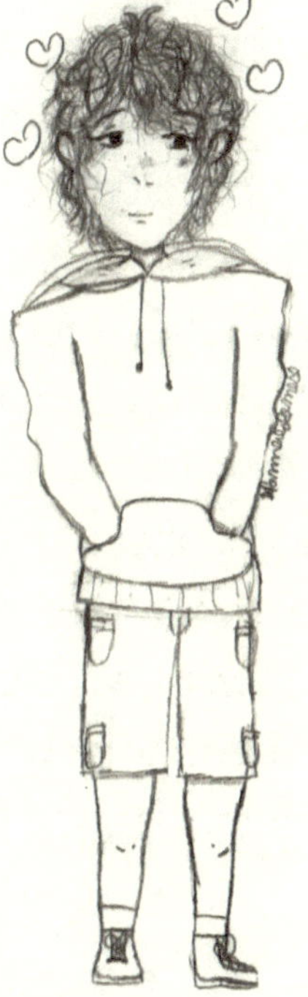

Hannah Jones

Taking It

Andrea Ramirez

If we get advice, do we take it? Or do we ignore it?
Or does it just depend on what the advice is?
Well, to me, advice is like a guideline.

The most advice that I would take is
From my brother and my parents.
It might be hard to take advice from someone
Who you rarely see, but I would.
Whenever someone you trust has actually
Experienced life more than you gives you advice,
Think about it and take it.

If it is for investment, a career,
Handling money, and life in general,
Take their word for it and try to follow the guidelines.
It might actually lead you to a great future.

It only takes a few minutes to take the advice,
But when you consider it,
You already have the right mentality.
Being it ahead of others at such a young age and
Already having a mindset of an adult.
There will be more to learn.
I really do think that if I take the advice and
Trust that person that good things will come.

There is a Fire

Alajah Thompson

"911, what's your emergency?"
"There is a fire.
And if we don't move fast,
It is going to kill all of us."

Heather thought to herself,
If we don't move,
We are going to die.
Turns out she didn't think to herself.

She said it out loud.
And everyone heard it.
Everyone started to freak out.
Chaos Stampede.

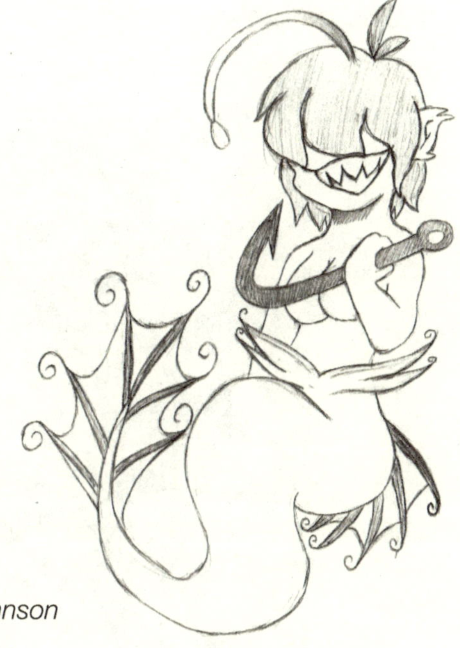

Teandra Johnson

Does It Feel Good?

Alajah Thompson

Does it feel good to
Be who you are?
Doing this and
Doing that all the time?

Not moving on a single bit,
Having to do what
Others tell you
To do all the time?

Having to be like this
It is the best thing ever.
You should be like them.
They should be like you.

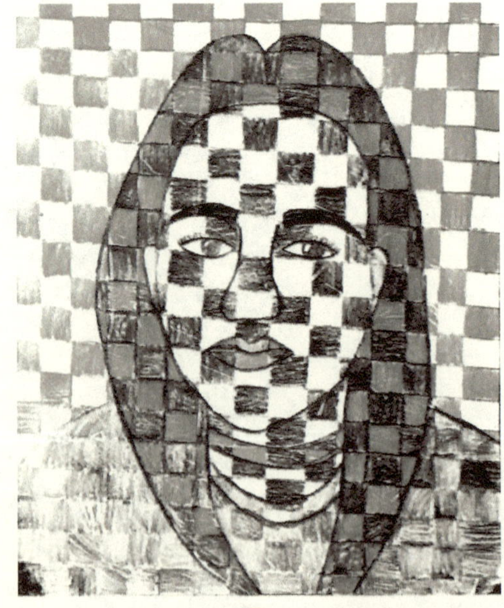

Cold Water

Da'Onna Watson

Cold water.
Freezing your fingers in an instant.
Thinking it will be fine enough to solve your problems.
It is relieving, but not enough.
Stick your shoulder in the water to relieve the pain.

10 seconds pass, cold.
20 seconds pass, cold.
30 seconds pass, cold.
Take it out, and it is numb.

Pain has the same effect.
You keep it for too long and it gets numb.
No more holding it in, tell someone.
Anyone.

But who is there to listen?

Perfectly Wrong

Danna Texis

I was told
Over and over again
That you were no good.
I defended your name.

I didn't want people's words to
Affect the way I cared about you.
You are the only person I've ever wanted.
My only addiction.

Sometimes your addiction can kill you,
But you still decide to run back or keep doing it.
Why?
Because you depend on it.

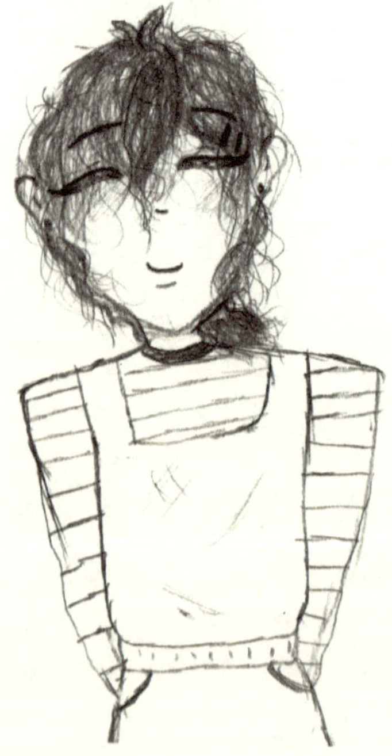

Hannah Jones

I felt like I needed you to stay afloat.
Without you, my life would have no purpose.
You were my absolute everything.
I cherished you like no other thing in life.

Although, the things that you hold
Most dear in life are the ones
You have to let go.
And that one thing was you.

I'm not sure if I'm fine.
Maybe I'm a mess,
But letting you go gave me awareness
To never depend on another person for happiness.
To put yourself first before another person.
To know my worth.

Lonely Boy

Ayden Sumaya-Beato

Sitting here feeling lonely,
Missing friends in the outside world.
Could it be that I'm the only
Boy who's feeling trapped in an isolation ward?

I wonder now about my friends.
Are their families making it through?
It feels like the world is at the end.
Could it be that this is true?

I know these feelings don't make me sound tough,
But at this point I'm not trying to be cool.
I never knew it would be so rough,
Without seeing my friends at school.

Letting our Forever Go

Danna Texis

My heart aches thinking about letting this go.
Us go.
The phase of Us
Will be left as if they never happened.
The memories will slowly fade, as I move forward with life
Although the love will stay,
Because it's you who I've loved so dearly.
And love as pure,
Dear,
That I had for you never goes away.
It stores itself into a special place
In my heart.
Only for you.

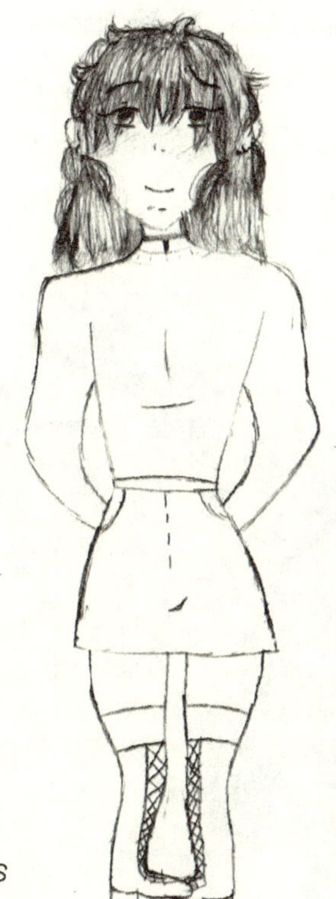

Hannah Jones

Party Until You Die

Ayden Sumaya-Beato

Why are people so dumb,
Ignoring guidelines meant to save?
People still trying to feel numb,
And living their lives like one big rave.

To stay away from friends and society,
Can help save lives of those at risk.
People act like their lack of sobriety,
Is worth more than lives of those who could get sick.

Stay away from those who're sick,
Stay away from those who're old.
Doing this isn't a trick,
And the benefits we will all behold.

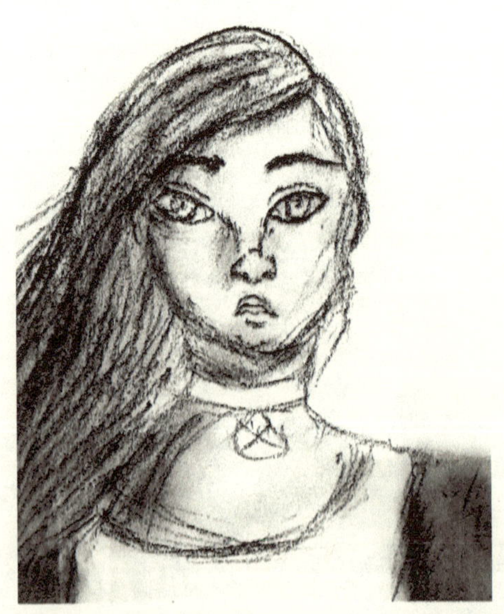

Worthy of Truth

Danna Texis

The truth speaks for itself.
Speaking the truth gets people to better places.
Resisting or holding back can be detrimental,
Although the truth can sometimes
Be the thing you live in fear of.

Does lying get you anywhere?
What comes from lying?
Consequences.
Then from that,
Regret.

If the truth were just to be spoken more often,
Mistakes could be more often avoid,
Although we are human.
The truth is what we run from.
There is no human on earth.
That does not fear the truth.

Logically Speaking

Ayden Sumaya-Beato

As I'm sitting here writing this,
I'm thinking of the things I miss.
With the phone and internet,
You may say things that you regret.

But, also with your body and your actions,
If only worried about feeling satisfaction.
So instead, be smart.. use your mind,
Follow the rules and stay in line.

No, it's not an act of treason,
But some things just stand to reason.
If you are only worried with how you feel,
There's no telling who your actions could kill.

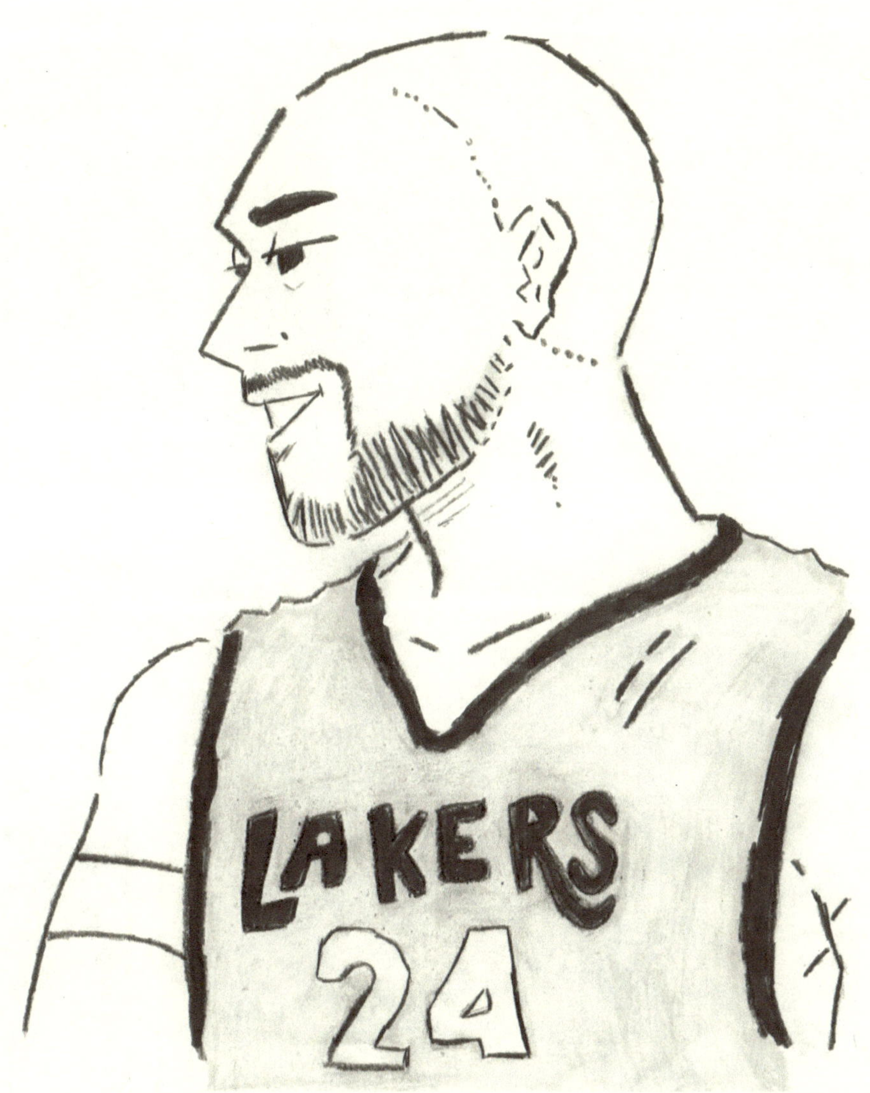

Antwan Chisolm

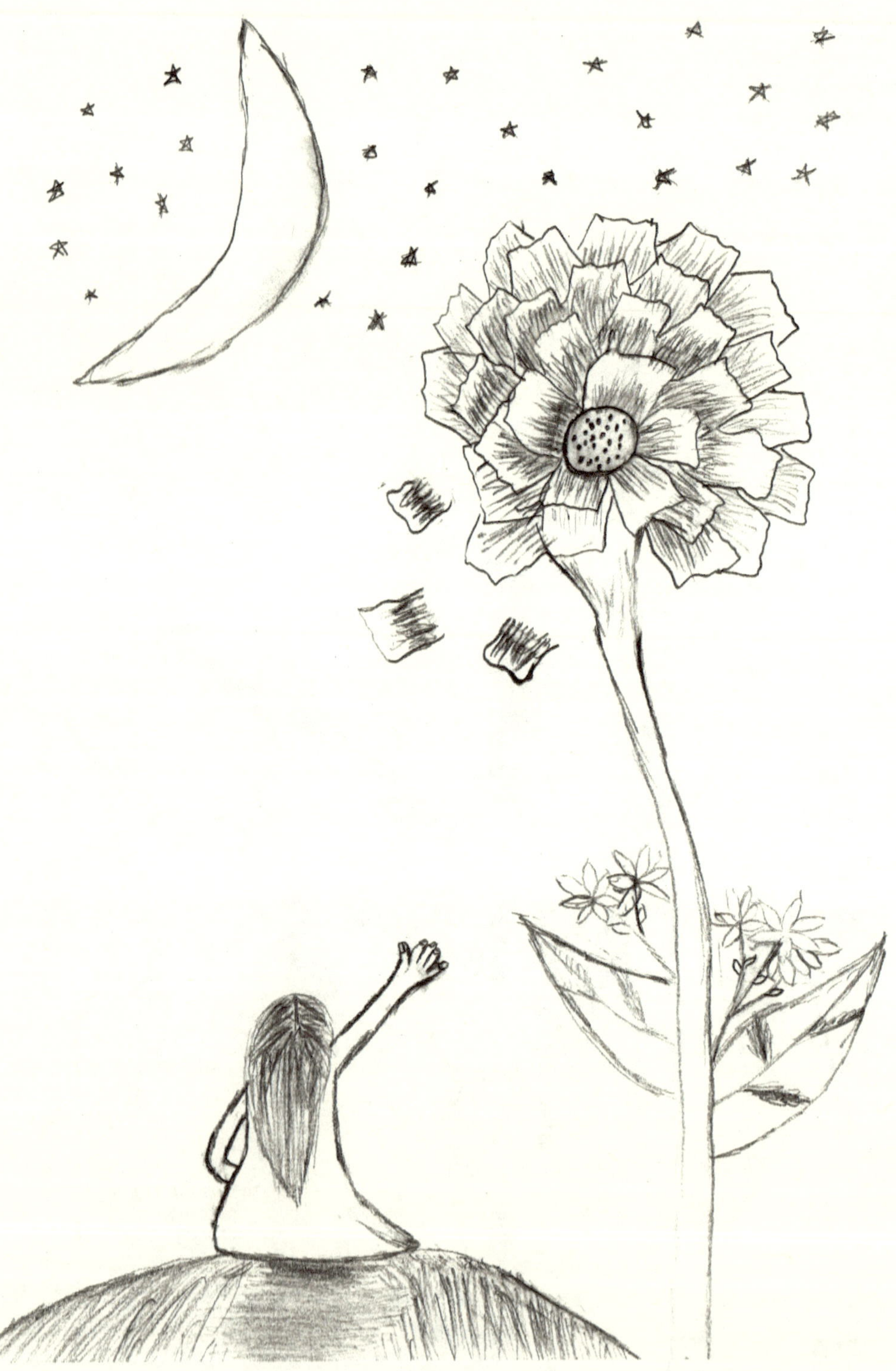

Angela Gonzalez

11 Random Haiku

Turn Into Spirit

Brandon Hernandez

My last freedom leaves,
Holding to the white branches,
Turn into spirit.

It Took My Future

Victor Santamaria

An outbreak that broke.
It took my privileges.
It took my future.

The Games

Jarreau Simmons

Doing my work sucks.
I would rather play the games.
Please, it's a bummer!

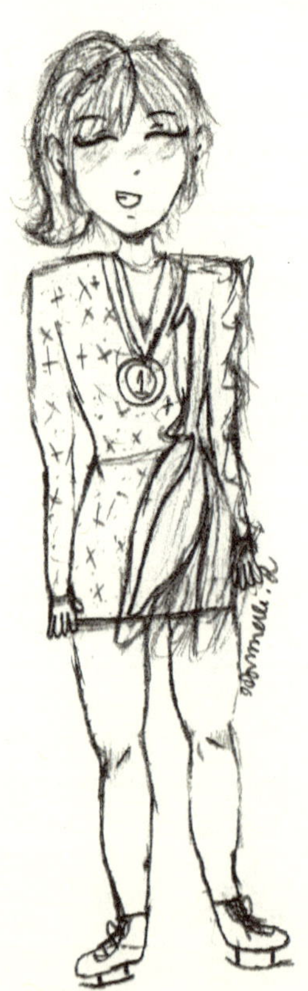

Hannah Jones

God's Punishment

Karoline Blanco

We are all locked up.
We all feel like prisoners.
Catch COVID-19.

Our Lives

Karoline Blanco

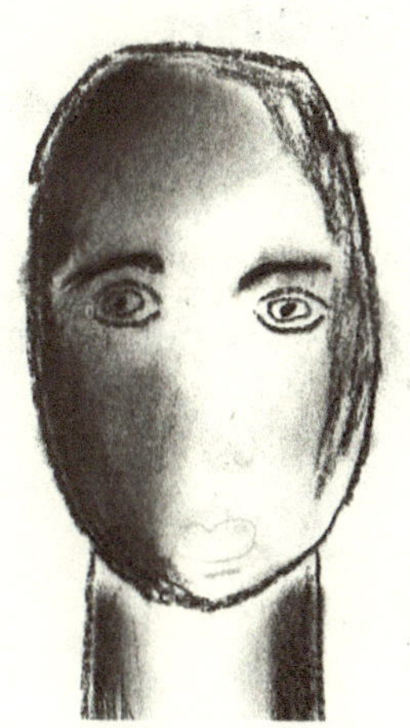

Staying in the house,
It was all a joke at first.
Our lives have changed now.

Hang In There

Karoline Blanco

Our school year is toast.
God says it's a punishment
Wait, let's hang in there.

Corona

NotJah'Sean NotBrown

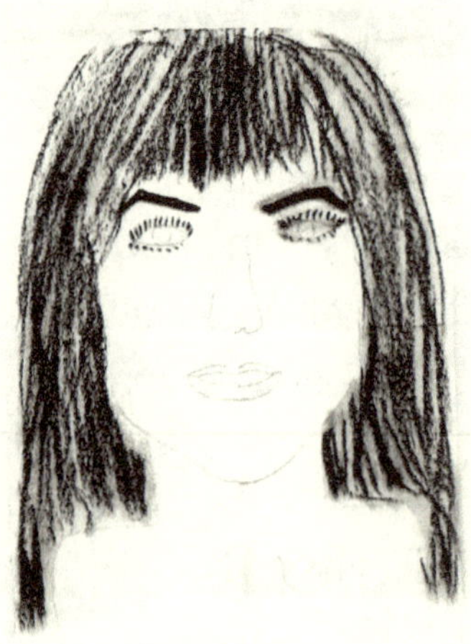

Come on, corona,
For everyone is waiting
For you to be done.

Everything is Different

Annabelle Lockridge

I should be at school.
My freedom has been stolen.
My freedom is gone.

To Be Free

Riley Metz

I want to be free.
I want to see friends again.
I want everything.

See You Soon

Shekynah Moore

Now we live in fear.
See you soon, humanity.
The end is coming.

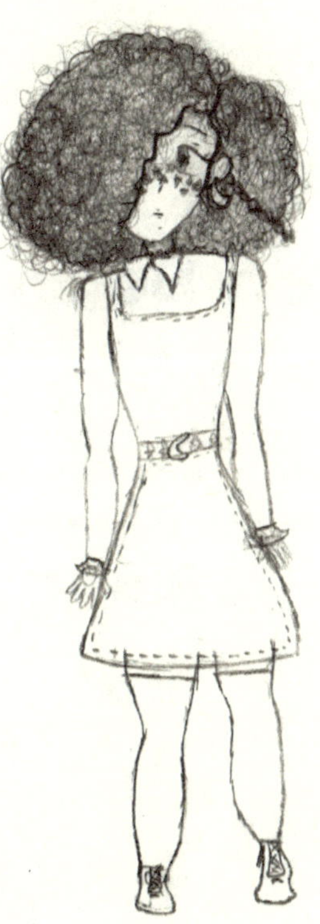

Hannah Jones

Stay Clean

Jose Ortiz

Stay clean! Wash your hands!
This can prevent many things.
Will it make you change?

New Beginning

Andrea Ramirez

The new beginning.
Everyone has a new start.
But who will take it?

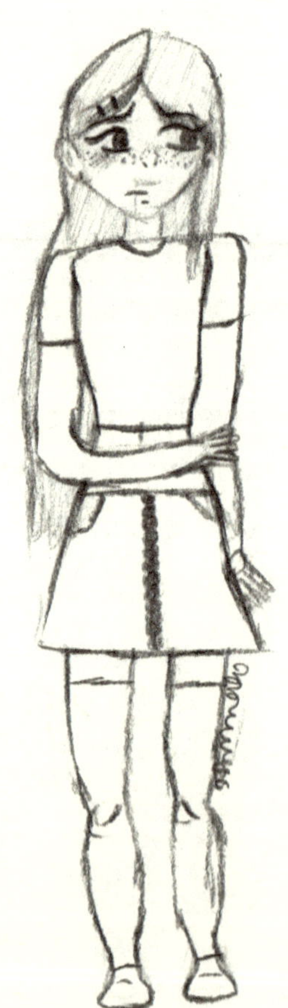

Hannah Jones

Wait To See

Andrea Ramirez

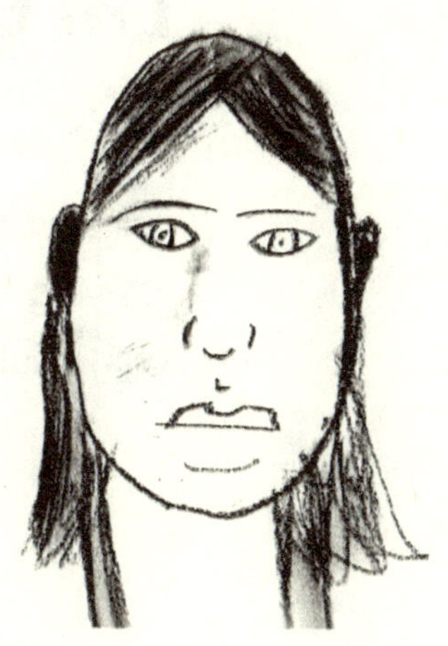

We'll just wait and see.
It's all a matter of time,
Just like the old times.

Living Got Harder

Bradley Perez

How will this turn out?
Will the world make a comeback?
Living got harder.

I'm Bored

Ayden Sumaya-Beato

This is boring me.
Staying inside every day.
Ugh, just kill me now.

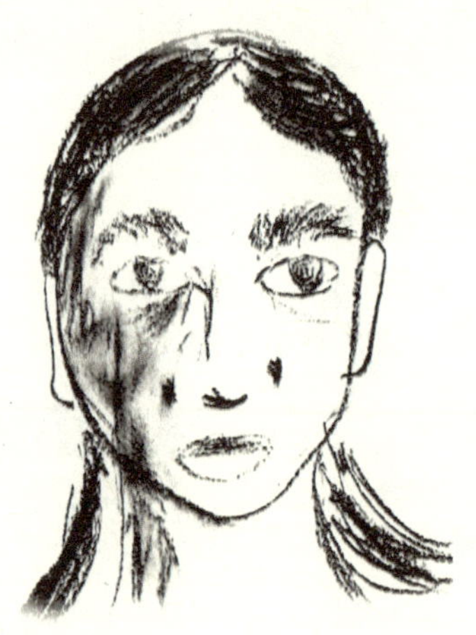

I Laughed

Ayden Sumaya-Beato

I laughed at people,
people who were wearing masks.
Look who's laughing now.

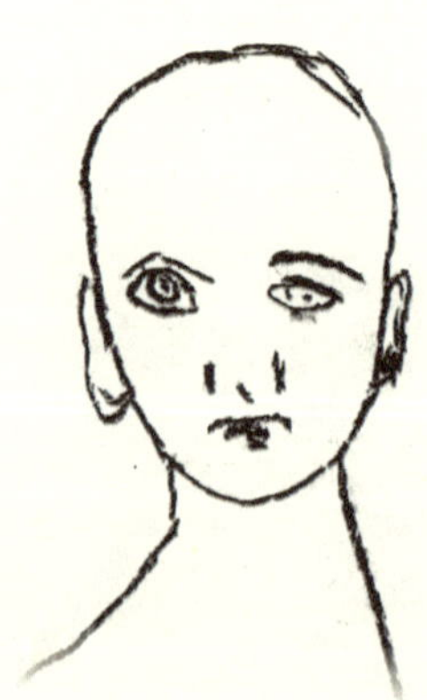

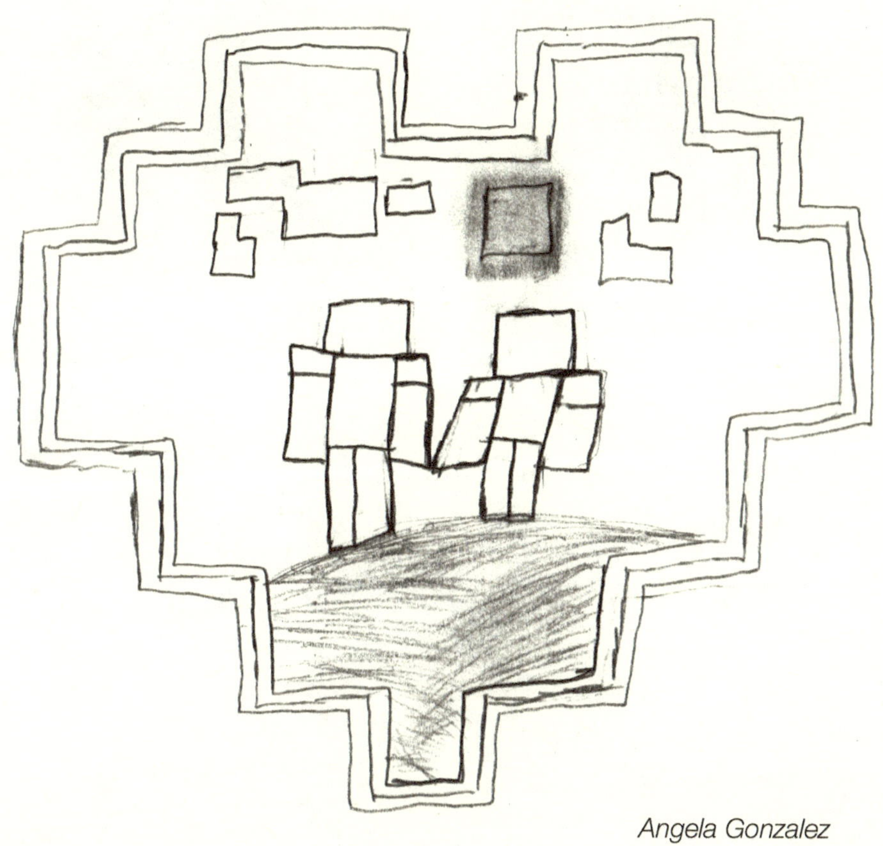

Angela Gonzalez

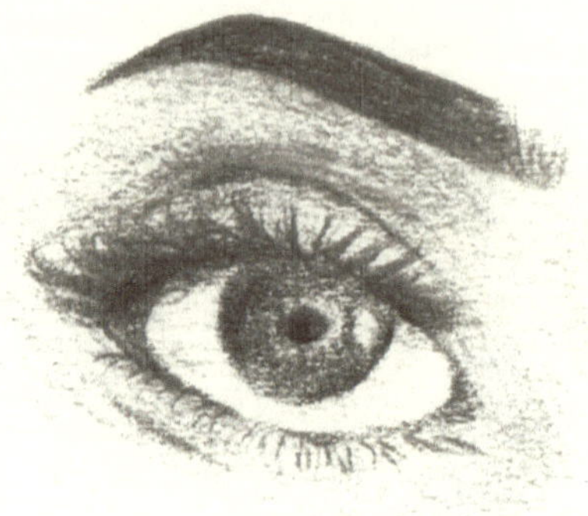
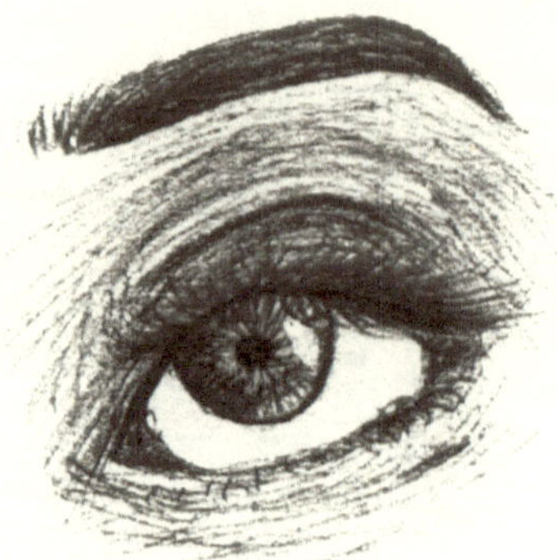

Addis Coronel

Epilogue

You know how sometimes things are just rolling along, no surprises, no emergencies, and everything seems okay? Pretty much every school year has been just like that. We drag on the second issue a bit. We pull it together at the last minute, finding artwork we didn't know we had, hammering out as much writing as possible. We recover from the post-Winter-break-slump just in time for Spring Break. We hammer through the testing season, which eats the month of May, and we enjoy the end-of-the-year activities we always treasure. The second volume of Zuckerbook is finished and rushed to the presses in the nick of time and distributed just after Memorial Day. After that, we organize the remnants of our work, back everything up, and watch the school year come to a triumphant end.

This year, things were a bit different. Winter break came to a close, and we returned to the halls of Zucker Middle School as we always do. The news mentioned some things about an illness going around in China. Sarcastic remarks were made. Then that illness started killing people in Europe. The sarcasm subsided, and questions arose. Then there were instances of the same disease documented on the West Coast, and concern was expressed. As time went on, students were concerned - for themselves, for their loved ones. Absences were noted and increased a great deal. Worried faces and wide eyes greeted me daily, disbelief at the news, and the data given.

Then, the nation seemed to explode with COVID-19. The faculty discussed what we might do if schools were closed. How will we maintain online classes for our students? How will we distribute technology? What can we do to make up the lack of essential services, such as food and tutoring, and access to the internet? On that Friday, March 13th, we sat down and created a plan for organizing our lessons, so everyone knew what everyone else was doing. We adapted our classwork to eLearning environments and stared at each other in disbelief. Would they really close schools across the state? Would all of the horrible things in America's major cities find their way to the Lowcountry?

School closed in the middle of weekly planning and grading the following Sunday afternoon. Why anyone was taken by surprise, I do not know. I sure was. I knew it was possible but didn't believe it would happen that fast. The plans we discussed and sketched just two days before were enacted the next day. Students were issued technology and books and work packets. Meal distribution began in nearby neighborhoods—Wi-Fi buses parked for hours in school parking lots. Online video conferences replaced classes. Students and teachers adjusted themselves to the new anything-but-normal. They pulled it together faster than anyone would be willing to believe, proving that we are the masters of our pedagogical domains and actually know what we are doing.

After the coronavirus closed everything down, the Murder Hornets came to terrify us all. Then, there was actual confirmation that UFOs exist. Then, the nation was set on fire, and the need for serious reform in law enforcement and civil rights was highlighted by a series of horrible tragedies that shook our community to its core and raised debates in all corners of the nation and eventually the world. Protests exploded into riots and looting. The spotlight shone cold on the relationship we have with our police, with our government, and with ourselves. We remain in the throes of that crisis as of this writing and wonder what could possibly follow.

We were only three weeks into Volume 12 of Zuckerbook when the schools closed. We had a lot of work done, but not all of it. The first Zuckerbook tee-shirts arrived the afternoon before the closure. We still needed writing and art to fill this book, lest we lose the funding we worked so hard to amass for the year. But the iMacs we needed were gathering dust in a classroom devoid of students, and everyone was frantically trying to stay on top of their work, student and teacher alike. It turns out that everything is a lot harder in an eLearning environment, even if you are technically doing fewer assignments. Everyone was exhausted, drained by the stress of quarantine, depressed by the lack of social interaction, feeling the walls close in.

Distractions became contagious. Students who were always at the top of their game in class vanished like a breath of wind. We spend as much time teaching as we did reaching out, sussing out who was in crisis and who let their flake flags fly. Classes like The Zuckerbook Project were suspended indefinitely.

So I was left with a tough decision that kept me up for many nights. What to do about Volume 12? I had enough material to get most of it done. I had plenty of artwork. I had lots of writing. Each year, we finish with leftover content, so even if I had to dip into that stash of writing from years gone by, it could be done. My students, early on, wrote poems about the pandemic; wrote sonnets after reading Romeo and Juliet; wrote haiku about whatever they wanted; and explored ways to use rhetoric in poetic form.

More than a few times over the years, dissatisfaction at the level of energy among The Zuckerbook Project Staff resulted in my saying that I could probably hammer out the entire volume by myself in just over a week. And, after the teaching was finished for the year, I was faced with a daunting reality: It was time to put my money where my mouth was and get this done.

Our archives were a teenage time machine of chaos. I try to step back as much as possible so that the kids can do most of the work, so peering into the lens of teenage workflow in mid-mindstorm was not easy. Typically, I struggle with whether or not to jump in. When I closed out the grade books for the year, it was time to have a seat and see if anything could be rescued.

It could. In some areas, we were farther along than I thought. In others, we barely began the process. Everyone involved did excellent work. That helped me a lot.

Not quite a week ago, I sat down at my iMac beast and began wading through Volume 12. I spent five straight days going through writing collected since the school closure. I combed through the work already edited. I pushed pieces of poetry through Grammarly to make sure they were authentic and scanned artwork I remembered to bring home last March. Of course, there was the inevitable struggle - I, as an English teacher, want to edit and clean things up way too much. Doing so means student voices get lost. We cannot have that. That's the entire point of Zuckerbook - let their voices be heard. Oh, what I heard as I plunged into the depths of the work we collected!

I found myself astounded at the quality of the writing they created. There is always brilliance in their writing, but this time the students outdid themselves. I worked their pieces into coherent chapters and stood back to have a look at what we had done.

It wasn't enough. We had a lot of the book, but we needed more content. So, a brisk breezing of work created at the end of the 2018-2019 school year brought about unpublished work from last year's wonderful writers. I found room for them, too, and after five consecutive ten-hour workdays, this volume is finished. I am very proud of my kids and thrilled to sit back and read it through.

There is no way to know how things are going to go next year. As of this writing, according to our administrators and the district, no less than eight different plans are being kicked around in the caverns of 75 Calhoun, each one with its own unique upside and a long list of downsides. I have been assured by those in the know that no one will like any of them and directed to keep an open mind, to be flexible, and to be available at least one week earlier than scheduled.

Okay, then. Off we go into the wild blue yonder...

In the meantime, I hope you enjoy Volume 12 of Zuckerbook and treasure it the way I have treasured it. I miss my kids terribly, lamenting how our school year coughed and sputtered and died, with no pomp and no circumstance. Reading through these pages brings their voices back to me and touches my heart. It is my hope that you feel the same.

With gratitude, a tip of the hat, and a big ole' smile,

Erik J. Hilden
June 7th, 2020

www.ingramcontent.com/pod-product-compliance
Lightning Source LLC
LaVergne TN
LVHW090937080826
845145LV00003B/783

* 9 7 8 0 5 7 8 7 1 7 0 9 8 *